THE FURTHEST POINTS

Motorcycle Travels Through Spain and Portugal

ANDY HEWITT

Contents

1. The Plan — 1
2. The New Plan — 9
3. The Day Before — 17
4. Day 1, 7 May — 25
5. Day 2, 8 May — 37
6. Day 3, 9 May — 47
7. Day 4, 10 May — 57
8. Day 5, 11 May — 69
9. Day 6, 12 May — 75
10. Day 7, 13 May — 81
11. Day 8, 14 May — 91
12. Day 9, 15 May — 99
13. Day 10, 16 May — 109
14. Day 11, 17 May — 119
15. Day 12, 18 May — 129
16. Day 13, 19 May — 139
17. Day 14, 20 May — 149
18. Day 15, 21 May — 157
19. Day 16, 22 May — 165
20. Day 17, 23 May — 171
21. Day 18, 24 May — 179
22. Day 19, 25 May — 185
23. Day 20, 26 May — 195
24. Day 21, 27 May — 203
25. Day 22, 28 May — 215
26. Day 23, 29 May — 225
27. Day 24, 30 May — 233
    Postscript — 239

    Appendix A — 241
    Appendix B — 245
    Contact the Author — 247
    Acknowledgements — 249

Copyright © Andy Hewitt, 2019

First Edition

The author asserts the moral right under the Copyright, Designs and Patents Act 1988 to be identified as the author of this work.

All rights reserved. No part of this publication may be reproduced, stored in a retrieval system, or transmitted, in any form or by any means without the prior written consent of the author, nor be otherwise circulated in any form of binding or cover other than that in which it is published and without a similar condition being imposed on the subsequent purchaser.

This memoir reflects the author's present recollections of experiences over time. Some events have been compressed, and some dialogue has been recreated.

This book is dedicated to Kim, my pillion through life.

1

The Plan

We were approximately halfway along one of my favourite roads. It starts at San Pedro de Alicante, which is just outside Marbella in Spain, and climbs 750 metres (2,500 feet) in elevation to where it finishes in Ronda. The road consists of 44 kilometres (27 miles) of glorious twists, turns, hairpins, sheer drops, cliff sides and, if you can dare take your eyes off the road for a few seconds, glorious vistas into valleys, gorges and mountains. A perfect biking road. The bike was fully loaded, with my wife, Kim, riding shotgun and enough luggage for an extended road trip. It was late afternoon, and after a long day in the saddle with miserable weather, I was getting a little tired but still feeling good as we drew closer to our destination.

It was cold and getting colder as we climbed the mountain into mist and drizzle caused by the low clouds that had been our companions for most of the afternoon. The roads were wet and shiny, and I thought I'd felt a bit of a shimmy from the tyres on a couple of occasions. I laid the bike into a right-hander, but she refused to follow the line I'd selected, and we drifted over the white line into the opposite lane. I instinctively felt that, if I laid her any further over, she would slide, and so, like an under-steering car, we drifted further onto the wrong side of the road, into the path of oncoming traffic and towards the sheer drop at the other side of the road...

How did we get into this situation? What were we doing here, risking life and limb? For this, we will have to go back to September of the previous year when Kim and I were sitting on our terrace enjoying an after-dinner bottle of Rioja, and the topic of conversation had turned to holidays.

'I want a proper holiday next year,' said Kim. 'We haven't had a proper holiday for a long time.'

'Hang on a bit. We spent Christmas and New Year in Dubai. In fact, we spent a whole month there.'

'Well, that doesn't count. You were working.'

'We drove from the UK to Portugal. That was a great trip. Remember how much we enjoyed Salamanca?'

'That wasn't a holiday either,' she said, folding her arms and tapping her foot. 'That was just you buying a new car and us driving it home.'

I continued to try and convince Kim that we did quite well for holidays, "proper" or not. 'We went to Cardiff to watch England play Wales in the Six Nations.'

'That was just a long weekend to watch rugby.'

'Well, on that trip, we also went hiking at Cheddar Gorge, and you like hiking,' I offered.

'Yes, I like rugby and hiking, but it was still just a long weekend and not a proper holiday.'

'We went to Marbella to stay with John and Michelle and then went with Yaz and Dava to Granada and Ronda. That was a week on the bike, and last summer, we had a week in York with Mads and the kids.' Maddie is our seven-year-old granddaughter and our "kids" are now both in their thirties.

'Yes, that was good, but after spending a week with Maddie, I needed a holiday to recover.'

'You've been to the UK to see your family a couple of times.'

'Ha! Well, watching daytime TV with my mom and dad is hardly a holiday, is it?'

'And we've only just come back from London. Apart the Aussies knocking England out of the World Cup, that was a good trip.'

'That was for Lisa and Warren's wedding and more rugby.'

I knew what she was getting at, of course. Since we'd moved to Spain two and a half years earlier and later settled in a house just over the border in Portugal, we'd done a lot of long weekends and short breaks but not what could be regarded as, well, a "proper" holiday. Mostly, I worked from my office at home, and I travelled on business quite frequently, but I didn't work anything like the hours I used to. I loved our new life in Portugal, and I pretty much regarded living there as one long holiday and appreciated the fact that we could take off for breaks to see places and to do things that weren't possible in our former life without them becoming major and expensive expeditions.

'OK then,' I said. 'What d'you class as a proper holiday? Where would you like to go?'

'China! I've always wanted to walk the Great Wall of China.'

'That's a long walk, and I'm with Karl Pilkington on that one. He says that, whilst you can see the Great Wall of China from space, you can also see the M62, but at least the M62 is useful. The Great Wall of China didn't even do what it was designed to do, which was to keep Genghis Khan and his marauding hordes out. Anyway, the Chinese eat weird food, and their sanitary conditions are less than ideal. I don't think you would like China.'

'Sri Lanka then! Sri Lanka is supposed to be beautiful.'

'I'm sure it is, but I've spent over twenty years living and working with a great deal of Asian people, so please forgive me if I don't fancy going to Asia for a holiday.'

'Machu Picchu! Now, that's amazing. I've always wanted to go there.'

South America had never been on my bucket list, but I thought I'd better show some interest. 'Where exactly is Machu Picchu?' I asked.

'It's on the Inca Trail, so it must be where the Incas come from.'

Lisbon the next, I have no idea, but we'd been to this event two years previously and, amongst several other acts, had seen the Rolling Stones. Mick, Keef, Charlie and Woody were totally brilliant, and as I had almost every Stones album in my collection but had never managed to see them play live, this was a major tick on my bucket list. This year, Bruce Springsteen, Queen (with Adam Lambert), Fergie, and The Stereophonics were all listed to play. I was up for both Bruce and The Stereophonics. I'm not madly keen on Queen, and I always thought that Fergie was Prince Andrew's former wife. Kim, who's a devotee of *American Idol, Britain's Got Talent* and all similar such shows, assured me that, although Adam Lambert didn't win any of these shows, he was nothing short of Freddie Mercury personified and that Fergie was a Black Eyed Pea and, therefore, very good. More compromise, I suppose.

Music is another area of difference between Kim and me. Music is one of my passions in life, and I've even played in a couple of bands in my time — nothing very serious, or to a very good standard, but I had fun with it. Whereas I'm a devotee of rock and blues, mainly of the seventies with iconic artists such as Jimi Hendrix, the Doors, Eric Clapton, the Stones, Led Zeppelin and the like figuring large in my collection, Kim prefers the type of music that featured on *Top of the Pops* in the days of Tony Blackburn, David (Kid) Jensen and Dave Lee Travis and "music that you can dance to, not like that slit-your-throat music of yours". Well, we're all different, thank goodness, and the upshot of all this was that *Rock in Rio* became part of the trip. This meant we would be setting off on 14 May, taking a couple of days to reach Lisbon, where we would meet up with friends from Spain who were also doing *Rock in Rio* on 19 and 20 May, before continuing on the road for the remaining two weeks or so.

When considering a route to Lisbon, I had fond memories of our trip to see the Stones. On this occasion, we'd also gone on the bike and had taken a couple of days to follow the Portuguese coast westwards along the Algarve, turned right when we reached the south-west corner and then headed north along Portugal's Atlantic West Coast. This had been a lovely couple of days' riding. The area

'Considering you've always wanted to go there, you don't seem to know much about it.'

'Well, you know I'm not much good at geography, smart arse.'

'I think the Incas all ended up farming cocaine, so it's probably in Colombia. It's a well-known fact that tourists always get kidnapped and held to ransom in Columbia, so that wouldn't be my idea of a holiday. Actually,' I said, with the benefit of a geography A-level, 'I think Machu Picchu is in Peru, which is a bit of a long way to travel. What about somewhere closer to home?'

'How about the States again then? We had an awesome trip last time we were there.'

This was very true. Ten years previously, we'd spent three weeks with our pals Kev and Moira touring California, Nevada and Arizona on a couple of Harley-Davidsons and had a truly memorable trip. The mention of our US trip piqued my interest, mainly because of the biking connection. Maybe Kim could be persuaded to consider a bike tour as qualifying as a proper holiday?

'Look. We've spent the last twenty years or so living outside Europe, so what about a European trip? We could even go on the bike,' I suggested, to see what sort of reaction the word "bike" would bring.

'Yes, that could work, but I don't want it to be all about the riding. I want to see things and do things as well.'

'We can do that,' I said, thinking that things were going in a positive direction now. 'D'you fancy an organised tour, or shall we just do our own thing?'

We'd previously taken part in a couple of excellent HOG (Harley Owners Group) official tours operated by Brettours and had a great time. On the first occasion, we'd flown to the UK from Abu Dhabi, where we were living at the time, collected a Harley-Davidson Electra Glide from London and joined the tour (along with about twenty or so other bikers) at Dover. After crossing the Channel, the superb Ron Brett, who's been doing this sort of thing for about twenty years, guided us along some brilliant biking roads through France, over the French, Swiss and Italian Alps and eventually to Lake Como in Italy.

We then returned via a different route. Fourteen days of terrific riding, great roads and excellent company. Each overnight stay was at a really good hotel, and we made stops for morning coffee, lunch and an afternoon break in the most picturesque of locations.

How Ron does it, I don't know, but he certainly does it well, and we couldn't fault anything at all. We enjoyed it so much that, a couple of years later, we repeated the experience with a seven-day Brettour of Normandy, Brittany and the Loire Valley. As the rest of the group headed for home, Kim and I carried on through France to the Spanish Pyrenees where we stayed for a week's hiking before returning northwards to drop the Harley off at Canterbury Harley-Davidson and then on to Heathrow for our flight back to the Middle East. This second tour was a good combination. We had one week of Brettours fantastic organisation, but then, as a contrast, during the second part of our trip, we were left to rely on our own devices. In some ways, choosing our own route, getting lost, deciding when and where we would stop for breaks and trying to find somewhere to sleep at night was a lot of fun. And whilst it can be a little frustrating, especially when trying to find accommodation at the end of a long day's riding, this sort of thing, to me at least, is more what bike touring is all about.

'The tours were a bit too regimented for me. I would have liked to stay longer in some places and see a few more things,' Kim said, echoing my thoughts. 'Let's do our own thing.'

'OK. I'm happy with that. Where shall we go?'

'What about Ireland? We've often talked about touring Ireland. Or even the UK.'

Both appealed to me. Ireland is a place I would love to see, and I'd spent hardly any time in the UK since we left those sceptred isles way back in 1992, but then I remembered the downside of biking in the UK and Ireland. Neither of these places are "green and pleasant lands" for no reason; and the reason for this is, of course, the weather. The thought of having a miserable time for two or three weeks because of the vagaries of the British or Irish climate didn't appeal very much. There was also the fact that it would take three or four days to reach the UK from our home in Portugal and the same to return which would take a big chunk out of the available time. I think it was then that I had the eureka moment.

'Hang on a bit. We've lived in Portugal for two and a half years now, and before moving here, spent a lot of time here, but we haven't even scratched the surface of Spain and Portugal. We've loved almost every place we've managed to visit. There's still the best part of two whole countries on our doorstep, waiting to be discovered. What about a tour of Spain and Portugal?'

'That sounds like a good plan,' Kim said, refilling our wine glasses. 'Let's do that then.' As usual with my beloved, there had to be a qualification. 'But I don't want to spend all the time on the bike. I want to see things and want to be able to have a few days off from riding when I want, or when we get to somewhere nice.'

'OK, we can do that. It doesn't have to be all about biking. When shall we go?'

'Well, not July and August, because I'll be busy with the apartment then,' she said. Kim was referring to a property investment we'd made several years before in South-West Spain. Whilst it had turned out to be a pretty crappy investment (due to buying it pre-world financial crisis), we'd benefitted hugely in other ways with many holidays and breaks spent there. The fact that we'd come to appreciate the area meant we'd moved to this region when it was time for us to relocate from the Middle East, where we'd lived for many years. When we relocated, we initially lived in the apartment whilst looking for a house. We eventually found a villa just across the border in Portugal. We still keep the apartment in the hope that it will eventually be worth what we paid for it, and this has provided Kim with a little business, running it for holiday lets. July and August are the busiest time for rentals, so Kim has to be on hand to welcome new renters and to get things spick and span when they leave and then ready for the next tenants. Conversely, however, this is my quietest time at work and the best time for me to take time off. Having said that, July and August can get pretty hot in Spain and Portugal, and this can be uncomfortable for motorcycling. Also, hotels would be expensive, and vacancies may be hard to find on the road because it would be during the main holiday season. Earlier or later, therefore, seemed to make sense.

'What about May then?' I ventured.

'OK.'

'How long?'

'Well, you need a proper holiday.'

'That's true. I haven't had more than a week off work at one time for about four years.'

'Let's make it two or three weeks,' Kim continued.

I thought about this for a while. I'd started my own business four years previously and never felt comfortable about taking long periods off work, but then I reasoned there isn't much point in running your own business if it doesn't allow you to enjoy life and, anyway, I would be able to keep in touch with the office via the Internet and phone. If there were any panics, the office would always be able to contact me.

'Right then. I'll block three weeks off work in May,' I said as I got up and headed towards the kitchen and the wine rack. 'This deserves another bottle.'

2

The New Plan

Having the basis of a plan, I did very little about anything until the New Year when, after returning from a day's ride, I realised that a couple of things on the bike needed sorting out for an extended trip.

We would be making the journey on Roadie, our Harley-Davidson Road King which I'd bought new, eight years previously. Standard Harley-Davidson seats have always left me with a sore backside on long rides, so I reckoned that, if we were to be covering a fair few miles, we deserved to do it in as much comfort as possible. I started to think about buying a new seat. I'd been considering that ever since I bought the bike but, as we'd not used this particular bike for any really long trips, it had remained on my things-to-do list. Roadie's windscreen was also looking a little worse for wear and had started to crack round one of the mounting points, so that could also do with replacing.

I occasionally thought about the trip and which route we would take, but inspiration wasn't forthcoming. The truth is that both Spain and Portugal contain so many fantastic places, most of which would be new to us; to take in absolutely everything would be impossible. Additionally, this was going to be a long trip, so I wanted to concentrate on places further afield than those within striking distance from home and which we could "do" over a long weekend or so. This ruled out a lot of Andalucía, and in any case, over the previous few years, we'd visited many of the must-see places in our locality, so the question remained — where did we want to go?

Madrid? No, been there, done that. Barcelona? Yes, definitely. Everyone says Barcelona is a magical place. The Pyrenees? We'd spent a week in the Western Pyrenees and found the area to be stunning. I'd also done a solo bike trip which included a very diverse route from France that had taken me over the Pyrenees and brought me out on the other side near Pamplona in Spain. I'd trusted to my instinct (and my new satnav) at the time, and I've never been able to remember the exact route, but it was magical. Andorra is in the Pyrenees, so how about putting that on the list? Why not, indeed?

I consulted Kim. 'Is there anywhere you'd like to visit on our trip, honey?'

'Yes, I'd like to go to Silves.'

'But that's only an hour or so down the road. We could go there any time.'

'You said we could go wherever I wanted, and I want to go to Silves. It looked lovely when we passed through it.'

Considering we'd spent a lot of time instilling into our children when they were younger that "I want never gets", Kim seems to be of the opinion that this doesn't apply between married couples. Whilst she did stop short of stamping her foot, I could see that, if the trip was going to be harmonious, I wasn't going to have it all my own way, and I was going to have to make some logical compromises for the sake of emotional ones. That's one of the differences between the two of us. I usually make logical, well-thought-out decisions after weighing up all the pros and cons and undertaking a detailed risk assessment, whilst Kim just wants to do stuff.

Sometime in the New Year, a friend mentioned that *Rock in Rio* was coming to Lisbon that year. Despite its name, it's a music festival that alternates annually between Rio de Janeiro and Lisbon. Why it isn't called *Rock in Rio and Lisbon*, or *Rock in Rio* one year and *Rock in* west of Lagos is beyond the package tour area of the Algarve and is very reminiscent of Cornwall. This coastal route gave me an idea. After Lisbon, why not continue to follow the Portuguese coast into Northern Spain, then east towards the Pyrenees along the Spanish Atlantic Coast; continue east through the foothills of the Pyrenees to North-East Spain, taking in Andorra on the way, and then follow the coast to Barcelona and then south-east along the coast to home? We could even fit in a visit to see our friends, Yasmin and David, who'd recently set up home in Denia, which is about halfway between Alicante and Valencia. This could be a complete clockwise circumnavigation of Spain and Portugal.

Warming to this idea. I suddenly had a new thought. Why not ensure it was a complete circumnavigation by visiting the extremes of the peninsula along the route? I jumped on the Internet and Googled extreme points of both Spain and Portugal. Wikipedia soon revealed that the extreme northern point of mainland Spain is Punta de Estaca de Bares in North-West Spain; the easternmost point is Cap de Creus, just south of the French border in North-East Spain; the most westerly point is Cap Touriñán, which isn't far from the northernmost point, and the extreme southern point is Punta de Tarfia, which is close to Gibraltar. Portugal has only one claim to fame in the Furthest Point stakes, and that is Cabo de Roca, near Lisbon, which also has the distinction of being the most westerly point of continental Europe, so that had to go on the must-visit spots too.

I submitted a proposal to senior management, and she seemed happy with the revised plan. Brilliant! That's the plan sorted then! Only, for various reasons, it didn't turn out like that.

Kim is allergic to all sorts of weird things. When we lived in Nigeria, we discovered she's allergic to bananas. On holiday in Rhodes, it was aubergines. In Bahrain, it was guacamole and, in Abu Dhabi, some type of nut caused a very extreme reaction. When we moved to Spain, it was pollen from a tree that's very common in the region and, in Portugal, it was processionary caterpillars. The allergies take different forms. The food-related ones cause her throat to constrict so that she finds it difficult to breathe, and the trees give her hay fever-like symptoms. I'm not even going to go into the caterpillar allergy, but suffice to say that, round where we live, in caterpillar season, it's not unusual to see a woman walking two dogs whilst dressed in a full HAZMAT suit.

Unfortunately, the house in Portugal that had become our latest home had what Kim refers to as a "pollen tree" right outside. I'm not sure what type of tree it is, but they are indigenous to this region, and when we both returned from a trip to Dubai, we found the tree was exuding its yellow pollen like a well-oiled machine, which, I suppose, is something it's designed to do. Suffice to say that Kim soon became pretty miserable, and I was almost deafened with the constant sneezing. Oh, yes, Kim has weird sneezes to go with the weird allergies. They start as normal sneezes, but the "oo" at the end of "atchoo" reaches supersonic frequencies. Kim says it's very uncomfortable for her, but both I and the dogs can vouch for the fact that it's not good on the ears of those who are in range either. The upshot of this was that, about a week and a half before we were due to leave, she wandered into my home office and said, 'Err, Lovey. Can we go on our holiday early, because I'm sick of this pollen thing?'

I thought about what I had to do workwise for a moment and realised that, if I got a few things squared away, it wouldn't be difficult for me to go earlier than I'd planned.

'Hang on a minute, though,' I said. 'What about the plan?'
'What plan?'
'The plan we've agreed. Set off in a clockwise direction round the coast, visit *Rock in Rio* in Lisbon and then carry on clockwise, past the Pyrenees and then follow the Spanish coast home, calling in to spend a few days with Yaz and Dava along the way.'

Bloody typical, I thought, *I've put all this effort into planning our trip, and Kim wants to throw all my organisation out of the window.*

The truth is that, apart from the basic ideas, all I'd done was buy a road atlas of Spain and Portugal from Amazon and look up the Furthest Points in the Internet.

'We're going to *Rock in Rio*, so if we leave a week early,' I continued, 'we'll have to reschedule the trip so we arrive there at the right time. We can't take a week and a half to get to Lisbon and then only have a week and a half to do the rest of Portugal and Spain.'

'Well, let's make that at the end of the trip then,' she said, showing somewhat uncharacteristic logic.

'Hmm. Let me have a look at timings and distances to see what we can do.'

I spent half an hour or so looking at maps, distances, travel times and a calendar and worked out that Lisbon would be about ten per cent of the approximate distance of the trip, but if we left a week early, we would be there about halfway through our timeframe. It wasn't going to be feasible to do *Rock in Rio*. I also wondered whether leaving one pollen tree behind would do much good when pollen trees are indigenous to the region, and there were bound to be other pollen trees en route. Mind you, I haven't been happily married for all these years without knowing when to pander to my darling's whims and, sometimes, somewhat illogical decisions. I'd spent the previous weekend giving Roadie a full spring-clean and polish and checked all her vitals, so I knew the bike was in good fettle and ready to go. I'd even ordered and received the new seat, complete with detachable and adjustable backrests for both rider and passenger. Luxury indeed. I'd ordered the new windscreen but was still waiting for delivery from the USA, but no doubt it would arrive before we were due to leave.

'OK, let's do it,' I announced, like the dutiful husband that I am.

As the departure date was now imminent, I thought I'd better review the plan and make a few more, umm, well, plans. *Rock in Rio* was now effectively out, so what remained on our must-do list would be to circumnavigate Portugal and Spain in a clockwise direction, taking in Andorra, Barcelona, the Furthest Points and a visit to Yasmin and David en route. Other than that, the plan was not to have a plan and to take each day as it came. That sounded like a great plan to me.

'Honey, when you were on the phone with Yasmin the other night for about two hours, did you ask if it would be OK to stay with them on the trip?' I asked.

'Err, I mentioned we would be going to see them but didn't discuss any dates because we didn't really know when we would be there. I'll check now.'

Kim and Yasmin can invariably find plenty of things to talk about, so it was some time later when Kim informed me it would be good if we could visit them on or around 10 May. Ann, one of Yasmin's friends whom we'd also got to know, would be visiting, and it would be great for us to be able to catch up with her.

'But that will only be four days into the trip. How the bloody hell are we going to get all the way round Portugal, the northern Spanish coast, the Pyrenees and halfway home again, not to mention visiting Andorra and Barcelona and doing four of the Furthest Points in four bloody days? We're going by Harley, not Concorde.'

'Well, we could always do it the other way round, couldn't we?'

So, there it was. Our original plan of travelling clockwise round the Iberian Peninsula had now become an anti-clockwise circumnavigation. Was it achievable? Only time would tell…

3

The Day Before

Owing to the "pollen trees", we'd brought our circumnavigation of the Iberian Peninsula (anti-clockwise) forward by one week. Before this decision was made, however, Kim had invited four friends for a dinner party which she'd arranged for the evening before our new departure date. Whilst Kim enjoys entertaining very much and makes an excellent job of hosting such occasions with all the bells and whistles, I fully expected her to phone our friends and cancel. After all, she had a very good excuse. But no, even though this meant she was going to have a pretty full-on day before we departed, she had no such intention. I had no idea how she was going to manage it all.

I was given orders the day before the dinner party to sort out everything I needed to pack for the trip. I'm pretty good at this type of thing because I've packed for business travel on a regular basis for several years. You won't catch me standing in front of my wardrobe with an empty bag and a confused look on my face, aimlessly selecting things I might need. Oh no! I use my tried and tested "list method". I developed it some years ago when, on almost every trip, I managed to forget something essential. On one occasion, I found myself in Singapore searching for an Apple shop where I could buy a dongle and remote PowerPoint slide-changer I needed for the next day. On another occasion, it was Johannesburg without cufflinks when I needed to be suited and booted. My phone charger was also regularly left behind. I now keep a list of everything I'm likely to need on a trip and simply check each thing off, either as I pack it or decide it's not needed on this occasion. I already had my usual list, but this needed supplementing to include clothing for a three-week motorcycle trip, so I sat at my desk and, starting with my feet and ending with my head, wrote down everything I thought I would need for both on and off the bike.

On several long bike trips over the years, I've found a range of clothing that works well for me, so let me share the benefit of my hard-won experience with you. Bike boots are good for, well, err, riding bikes, I suppose, and I have a great pair of cowboy-style boots I usually use. Unfortunately, however, bike boots, by their very nature, tend not to be good for walking in. Consequently, if you find yourself stopping in a quaint little town that deserves further inspection, such an excursion can soon become an uncomfortable experience. I'd invested, therefore, in a pair of good old Doc Marten boots for the trip. I'd used these before, and they make excellent boots for both biking and walking, fulfilling the necessity that multi-purpose items such as these are the secret of good packing for a bike trip.

Shoes for size 11 feet take up a lot of luggage room, so Kim warned me that only one extra pair of shoes would be allowed. I plumped for a pair of trainers on the basis that they would be comfortable for off-bike sightseeing days, could be used for what they were designed for, i.e. keeping up with my exercise regime (which I didn't), and they would also just about be acceptable attire for restaurants and the like in the evenings. On reflection, maybe the shocking blue and lime-green pair that I use in the gym weren't the ideal choice because they rather spoiled the sartorial elegance I try to adopt when dining in smart restaurants. Not for me the Englishman-abroad look of formal socks with everything, including sandals. I select my socks with care. Consequently, pairs of long, warm socks for riding, formal socks for evening and sports socks for wearing with shorts completed the feet part of the packing list. A pair of Levi's, a pair of shorts and gym / swimming shorts would take care of the leg department.

As any serious outdoors type will tell you, the secret of maintaining a comfortable body temperature no matter what the weather throws at you is layering. My base layer is a Climalite T-shirt. You can forget the cotton T-shirts with "I Have Been to This or That Harley Dealer" on the back. Most people won't believe you anyway, and cotton isn't good for washing on the road; it creases when packed, holds the moisture when you sweat and, thus, gets somewhat unsavoury in hot weather. The Climalite shirts wick away moisture (what does "wick away" actually mean anyway?) are impossible to crease and, if they've done a lot of "wicking", can be hand-washed in a hotel bathroom and will be dry by morning. Layer two is a long-sleeved thermal shirt to keep me snug in cool weather. Layer three is a thinnish thermal fleece for similar reasons which can also be used off the bike. With the addition of my bike jacket and waterproof over-jacket, this makes five layers to put on or take off as necessary.

Just about the only situations where I've been uncomfortably hot were occasions in the Middle East and Arizona where I was riding in temperatures rising to 50°C (120°F). I know the Arizona temperature was correct because the air temperature gauge on my rented Electra Glide was hard against the stop at 120° F (50°C) and because it was bloody hot. As for the cold, I haven't lived in cold countries for many years, so memories of being frozen on a bike go back to my earlier biking days when I was either too poor or too stupid to invest in decent riding gear.

Anyway, a couple of casual shirts and a couple of T-shirts would do for evenings and non-biking days, so that was my upper body taken care of. With the addition of a few toiletries and odds and sods such as electrical chargers, that was my packing just about taken care of. It took about ten minutes for me to collect it all together and place it in a surprisingly small pile for Kim to pack away in our touring bags.

I also spent a few minutes making sure my riding gear was all present and correct. I like to wear jeans when riding but, being safety conscious, as well as wanting to cut a dashing figure on my Harley, I have for years worn Kevlar-lined Draggin' Jeans, which offer protection against gravel rash in addition to looking much better than the baggy touring pants that BMW riders wear. Bikers amongst you may have seen the advertisement for Draggin' Jeans, the one with the guy sitting on the tarmac being towed on his backside by a pickup truck and suffering no apparent aftereffects. I do, however, wonder what protection they would offer if the pickup driver suddenly jammed on the brakes.

I intended, however, to take my recently purchased Bull-It Jeans, which have the same protective properties as Draggin' Jeans but with the added benefit of being water-repellent. This should make them ideal for spells of light rain when it doesn't warrant stopping to put on waterproofs, but if you don't, you end up with damp legs. The trip would probably be the first opportunity to test just how true the maker's water-repellent claims were.

Obviously, you need something to keep your jeans from falling down, and I have my special "biking belt". This is a souvenir from the States where it was purported to be hand-made by Native Americans and features a design incorporating silver conchos and a silver, engraved buckle. I later had my suspicions about it being a genuine Native American artefact when I saw a delivery being made to a tourist shop in Nevada, which sold similar items, and I noticed that "Made in China" was stamped on all the boxes.

I have a problem with waterproof over-trousers. I'm a tall bloke, but most of my height is in my torso, so I don't have particularly long legs. Despite this, every pair of waterproof over-trousers I've owned are too short in the leg and, when on the bike, leave anything up to three inches of jeans exposed to get soaking wet. Now that I'd moved back to a wetter place, I was determined to find a pair that fitted properly. In a large biker shop, I tried a pair in my size. Not bad but, as usual, too short. I tried the next size — very big on the backside and still too short. The next size — you could have got two of me in them, but they were still the same length. I eventually ended up buying the too-short-but-fit-me-round-the-waist pair.

My bike jacket is a brilliant piece of kit from Harley-Davidson known as a Switchback, made from Cordura-type nylon, with an inside mesh lining. It has body armour on the shoulders and elbows, front and back vents for temperature control, more pockets than you will ever need and — here is the great feature — the outer panels can be unzipped and removed for hot weather to leave a vented mesh jacket which still retains the armour.

If things get wet or chilly, I can bring out my fifth layer of upper-body wear, which is my trusty Frank Thomas waterproof jacket. It's comfy, has always done what it says on the tin, and in dry but cold weather, it can also add a further wind-proof layer to help to keep me toasty.

In the hope that my hard-won experience of packing for a bike trip will be of some benefit to others and hopefully save someone from a lot of head scratching, I've included a copy of my packing list at the end of the book. I did ask Kim if she had any handy hints for lady bikers, but all I got was the advice that a sports bra helps to keep things in place on rough roads and cobbled streets; a pashmina can be used to accessorise an evening outfit and, if worn under a bike jacket, will also keep you warm and, oh yes, always keep your lippy handy. I did, however, persuade her to make a list of the things she packed for the trip, and this is also included at the end of the book.

Kim doesn't really do lists, but if she did, her things-to-do list for the day before our departure would look like this:

Take dogs for morning walk
Go to Pilates
Go shopping for dinner party
Go to post office and queue for forty minutes to buy stamps, post letters and pay electricity bill
Go to bank to get some cash for trip
Take dogs to kennels
Prepare food for dinner party

Clean and tidy house from top to bottom. (I have no idea why she does this, because the first thing she does when she gets home after an absence is to clean the house from top to bottom)
Clean outside of the house, front and back (similar observations as last item)
Make sure pool is topped up with chemicals
Water plants, indoors and out
Pack gear for the trip
Get best plates, glasses and cutlery out and set table for dinner party
Prepare and cook three courses for dinner party
Have shower, get made up and dressed for dinner party
Host dinner party
Clear table after dinner party
Wash dishes etc.
Put away best plates, glasses and cutlery.

As well as not doing lists, Kim tends not to do too much pre-planning. As a person who likes to pre-plan things a lot, during the preceding few days, I'd checked Roadie's oil levels and tyre pressures, given her a wash, fitted the luggage rack and still-broken windscreen because the new one hadn't yet arrived, made sure that everything that was supposed to be in the pannier where I keep the bike stuff was all present and correct and, finally, sorted out and checked my riding gear. Consequently, I had a somewhat shorter list:

Go to gym
Finish off a few things for work
Have chat with the office
Uncork a few bottles of red
Select playlist on iTunes for suitable dinner party ambience
Make sure everyone's glass is topped up during dinner party.

I don't know how she did it, but Kim managed to get everything done, looked gorgeous by the time our guests arrived, and the dinner party was enjoyed by one and all. We said goodbye to our guests around midnight and, wanting to be bright-eyed and bushy-tailed in the morning, I went to bed, leaving Kim relaxing on the terrace, polishing off a bottle of champagne. I guess she deserved it.

Roadie, spick and span and ready for the trip

4

Day 1, 7 May

Route: Home — Seville — Jerez de la Frontera — Vejer de le Frontera — Tarifa — San Pedro — Ronda
Distance: 506 kilometres (324 miles)
Distance so far: 506 kilometres (324 miles)
Bike time: 7 hours 30 minutes
Overnight: Hotel Catalonia, Ronda

The next morning was the start of our trip. I was awake at 7:30, had eaten breakfast, showered, dressed, got my riding gear out and was ready to hit the road by 8:30. *Yay, let's do it! Come on, let's go!* By nine o'clock, however, my beloved was still wandering round in a towel (I don't know why she does this when she has a perfectly good bathrobe), tidying up the house (which was already perfectly tidy to my bloke's way of thinking), watering the plants again, putting the contents of a chemist's shop in a Ziploc bag and finishing packing. I was sitting on the terrace with another cup of coffee and a cigarette, trying to remain calm, when the cry came from upstairs. 'Lovey! I can't get all this stuff in the bag. We'll have to use the other one as well.'

'I thought you'd packed yesterday, and it all fitted.'

'I did, but I just thought that, when we stay at Yaz and Dava's, we'll be going out to dinner. Yaz and Ann always dress well, so I just thought of a few more things I'll need to take. Anyway, just get the other bag, will you?'

A while later, Kim told me that the bags were now packed, so I could put them on the bike as Kim was almost ready.

The touring bag is another neat piece of kit. It rests on the luggage rack and has a pocket that fits over the sissy bar and has straps that attach to the rack to keep it securely in place. With one large compartment and three outside pockets, it holds a surprising quantity of stuff. There's also a smaller bag that straps on top of the main bag, but I'd forlornly been hoping we wouldn't need this one. The last piece of luggage was a bag which is purpose-made to fit neatly inside Harley touring bikes' panniers so that, when you reach your destination, you just lift the bag containing your stuff out of the pannier as opposed to having to juggle with a loose collection of things and drop them all over the car park.

The Road King has sizeable panniers, one which is for the luggage bag, and the other is pretty much permanently packed with bike gear including our waterproofs, a small tool roll, a first aid kit and one of those aerosol puncture repair things that are full of gunk. I've owned the puncture aerosol for so long that all the paint, including the instructions, has worn off from constant rattling round in the pannier, so it's probably well past its sell-by date. Still, this just goes to prove my theory that, if you carry such things with you, you'll never need them, but if you don't have them with you then, in the remotest place possible, where there's no phone signal, you'll get a puncture or some other disaster for which you're not equipped, and you'll suffer a lingering death. Well, I'm still alive, so it's worked out OK so far.

Bags installed and bike gear on, I was now champing at the bit. By now, however, what had started as a sunny day had turned to grey skies and drizzle. Looking over the river towards Spain, where we would soon be heading on our anti-clockwise route, the skies were even greyer. *Shall I put on my wets or chance it?* I hate putting waterproof pants on, especially when I'm already wearing my boots. *Bugger it, I'll chance it.*

Kim made an appearance at around a quarter to ten. 'Are you ready then?' she asked. 'You said we had a long way to go today, so let's get a wriggle on.'

'Yes, dear!'

Eight minutes later, we were crossing the River Guadiana into Spain. Another country, another language and, weirdly enough, especially for those of us who live close to the border, another time zone. Due to the time difference between the two countries, we had set off from our house in Portugal at quarter to ten and arrived in Spain eight minutes later at seven minutes to eleven Spanish time.

The first leg of our journey was to Seville. We'd travelled this road many times, not to visit this beautiful and historic Moorish town with its wide river and oranges, but to get stuff from IKEA when we were first furnishing our apartment in Spain and, more recently, our house in Portugal. So now, we were heading back to IKEA, sorry, Seville, on the Harley and, as usual during the first twenty minutes of any journey, I was settling into the ride and discovering all those things that become apparent only when you're on the bike and you can't do much about them. It was cold, and I had a draught up my sleeve. No problem, just tighten the Velcro on the cuff of my jacket. The Doc Martens were a lot shorter than my usual biker boots, so I also had cold draughts blowing up my trouser legs. Well, I wasn't going back to change them, so I resolved I would have to live with draughty legs for the next couple of weeks. *The strap on my helmet needs tightening a bit.* Mental note to do it up at the first stop. *I'm quite cold.* Another mental note to put my fleece on under my biking jacket at the next stop.

Eventually, I settled into the bike, sat back, relaxed and began to feel that marvellous sense of, as they say, being at one with the machine. This is a feeling that's pretty much unique to a motorcycle in that, unlike a car where you're essentially a passenger in a metal box that can almost drive itself, the rider becomes a *part* of a motorcycle. The way you sit, the way you balance yourself on the bike and the way you apply the controls are all necessary functions that change an inherently unstable machine into a functioning mode of transport because, without a rider, a motorcycle is essentially just a collection of parts that, if it didn't have a kickstand to support it, would fall over when not moving.

Raising the cruise control, which most touring bikes have these days, to a steady speed of 130 kph (80 mph), I patted Kim's leg to let her know I was happy and started to think about what lay in front of us. This didn't take very long because, apart from the Furthest Points, a visit to Denia to see Yasmin and David, Barcelona and Andorra, we didn't have a plan at all. That's the best part about this type of road trip. We'll see what happens when we get there but, after at least a couple of hours of meticulous planning, the journey had begun.

The route to Seville is via a motorway. 'Oh no,' I hear you say whilst mentally picturing the M25, M1 or M-whatever. 'A motorway on a bike!' This is not the case, however. The motorways in Spain are generally nothing like the motorways in the UK or other densely populated countries. Apart from those that surround the major cities, they're generally dual carriageways. They don't have a lot of traffic on them, and they mainly travel through countryside as opposed to urban sprawl. In short, whilst not being the fast A-roads with sweeping bends that bikers dream of, they're not a bad way to travel at all, and they mean you can cover a good distance whilst still enjoying the journey. Try doing that in most parts of the UK these days. Last year, it took me five hours to travel by car from Watford to Gatwick via Ealing, a total distance of 144 km (89 miles), which works out to an average speed of just 22 kph (14 mph). This was about the same distance as it is from home to Seville, and we arrived in Seville about an hour and twenty minutes after setting off, making our average speed 105 kph (65 mph).

Ignoring the advice of Satnav Woman, who is the rathar posh

lady who lives in my GPS and who, on a previous trip, had cleverly worked out that the best route to the far side of Seville is in a straight line through the congested city centre (which it isn't), we took the ring road round the city, over the River Guadalquivir and were soon heading out of Seville towards Jerez de la Frontera and Cádiz.

The River Guadalquivir is interesting for two reasons. Firstly, it's big, so it allows large ships to reach Seville from the Atlantic under the nose-bleedingly high bridge that we'd just traversed. When we moved to Spain from Dubai, our personal effects, including Roadie, were delivered to Seville in a 12-metre (40-foot) container. Secondly, despite Seville being roughly 100 kilometres (62 miles) from the coast, there appear to be no bridges across the river between Seville and the estuary. Imagine living in Sanlúcar de Barrameda, which is where the river enters the Atlantic. If your grannie lived at the other side of the river, you would probably be able to wave to her across the water, but you would need to take a 400-km (250-mile) round trip just to pop in for a cuppa.

Anyway, twenty or so minutes after entering Seville's western suburbs, we were exiting Spain's fourth largest city via the suburbs on the south side and on our way south-west. Think about this for a moment. Seville has a population of 703,000. Glasgow, which is the UK's fourth largest city, has a population of 600,000. England's fourth largest city happens to be our home town of Sheffield, which has a population of 520,000. What are the chances of getting from one side of Glasgow or Sheffield to the other in twenty minutes? The Spanish do road systems very well.

Leaving Seville behind, it was time for gas and coffee, so we pulled into a service station where I filled up the bike whilst Kim wandered across to the restaurant to order coffees and cheese and ham toasties. Just the job and something that was to become somewhat of a staple diet for the next three weeks.

Back on the bike, we had a choice of two routes heading towards the South Coast and Cádiz — the A-4 or the N-IV, both of which we'd travelled on several occasions. The A-4 is a two-lane A-road, and the N-IV is a motorway toll road. The A-4 is more interesting for riding, but it tends to be used by trucks and older cars who don't want to pay the tolls. On other occasions, I would have taken the pretty way and trusted Roadie to get us past any bottlenecks of traffic, but on this occasion, we had some mileage to cover (even though we're in Europe, I don't think I can say kilometrage), so I opted for the toll road. The route took us round Jerez de la Frontera, where the Spanish Moto GP is held, and turning left before Cádiz, we were soon following the coastline in a south-easterly direction towards our first Furthest Point at Tarifa.

After leaving the Cádiz area, the road turns into a fast A-road which winds through some spectacular scenery of varying altitudes. At one point, Kim tapped me on the shoulder and pointed out the purple wildflowers that carpeted the whole countryside. Gorgeous! Unfortunately, at about this point, the grey clouds that had been building for a while became blacker, and on feeling the first spots of rain, I stopped so that we could put on our waterproofs. Soon, we were riding through pretty heavy rain, but this wouldn't be for long as our next stop was only about 20 kilometres (12 miles) away.

Approaching Tarifa, there's a section of coast that's quite unspoiled. The beach is a long, continuous strip that runs for several kilometres and is bordered by pine forests. The Spanish authorities, in their wisdom, seem to have restricted the kind of development which has spoiled so many of Spain's costas. Possibly the area is a national park, but whatever the reason, the few hotels there are quite small and seem to hark back to a bygone age, and the only residential properties seem to be for the local population, as opposed to tourist or holiday-home developments. All this means that this stretch of coast remains blessedly natural and unspoiled. We'd been here a couple of times before, and on a previous visit, we'd stayed at the Hotel Dos Mares, an oldish but delightful boutique hotel on the beach. We'd enjoyed much better weather conditions on this previous occasion and had spent several hours chilling on the beach, watching the many wind- and kitesurfers that favour this stretch of coast, their multi-coloured sails creating a kaleidoscope of colour over the sea.

Apparently, the Straits of Gibraltar create a funnel effect which concentrates both the westerly or easterly winds, and it makes this area one of the most popular destinations in the world for wind- and kitesurfing. That would explain the preponderance of VW camper vans.

The Hotel Dos Mares was to be our lunch destination, and we arrived at 3 p.m. for, what I suppose by that time, was something of a late lunch. We ate in the restaurant at the side of the beach which, in more clement weather, would have had the glass sliding doors open to become an al-fresco dining area. That day, the weather was bleak. There were no kitesurfers to be seen, and we were glad to be in the warm and dry with the sliding doors closed.

An hour later, we were back on the bike. The rain was less heavy now, but as Peter Kay would say, it was "that fine rain that soaks you through", so we were dressed in our wets again. About fifteen minutes later, we were entering Tarifa and heading towards the Punta de Tarifa. Tarifa is a quirky little town which has quite a hippy / surfer vibe to it, but this time we didn't linger and headed straight to the town's southern tip. It's also the southernmost point of the Iberian Peninsula and continental Europe. This last point surprised me because I expected that either Italy or Greece would claim this geographic accolade.

As the Furthest Point South, it was also our reason for being there. The point itself lies on Isla de Las Palomas, a small island lying offshore which is connected to the mainland by a causeway. As well as being the Furthest Point South, Punta de Tarifa happens to qualify for two more interesting statistics. Firstly, it's situated at the narrowest part of the Straits of Gibraltar. The African coast is just 14 km (8 miles) away, and the mountainous coast of Morocco can be seen clearly from this point, even on a dull, overcast day such as the day that we were there. Secondly, Punta de Tarifa is also the place where the Mediterranean Sea meets the Atlantic Ocean, so if you go for a paddle on the Western side of the causeway, you'll be paddling in the Atlantic and probably have very cold feet, but if you paddle on the eastern side, you'll be in the

Mediterranean with lovely warm feet. We didn't test my theory, however.

Our first Furthest Point ticked off, we were on the Harley again and following the coast heading north-west. We passed the port town of Algeciras, where ferries leave regularly for journeys between Spain and Morocco (so that's how the Moors arrived there!) Looking to our right, the Rock of Gibraltar was visible through the misty skies. We'd been to Gibraltar a couple of years previously when we were holidaying at our apartment. I'm a bit of a history buff and have a particular interest in the Napoleonic Wars, so I had long been keen to visit what has become a symbol of Britain's overseas power and particularly its naval superiority during this era. Whilst we were glad we'd done the trip, we did leave feeling underwhelmed by the experience. It may once have been a proud outpost of the British Empire, thumbing its nose at the Spanish just across the causeway and controlling all shipping that attempted to pass along the straits, but these days it looks somewhat down at heel.

After wandering round for a while, the novelty of British bobbies, Union Jacks, red telephone boxes and pillar boxes soon wore off, and all that remained seemed to be Asian-owned off-licences, Red Lion pubs (as if there aren't already enough of those on the Spanish costas) and tacky souvenir shops. Apparently, a major source of Gibraltar's income these days is the hosting of Internet gambling sites because these cannot be hosted in mainland UK. It all seemed a bit seedy somehow.

We did the tourist things — the caves and the tunnels excavated by the British Army during the Great Siege of 1779-83 form part of what is arguably the most impressive defence system anywhere and were quite awe-inspiring; the flea-bitten and bad-tempered monkeys less so. There were only about three hotels in Gibraltar at the time, all of which had grim reviews on TripAdvisor, so we'd rented a cabin on a boat as guests of the owners and permanent occupiers, which was a different, if somewhat cramped, experience.

Gibraltar had been worth a visit just to see what it was like, but we wouldn't be rushing back there. I did leave with a good feeling, though. Not because of the place itself, but because I managed to get one up on the system, which in my mind is always a good thing.

Parking, as you might imagine in such a densely populated area, is a bit of a nightmare, so after failing to find anywhere, I eventually parked in a ticketed car park and accepted that, two-and-a-bit days later, when we were due to leave, we would be looking at a hefty fee. Returning to collect the car, I noticed that, on the sign displaying the car park rules (how very British), it clearly stated that, if you lost your ticket, you would have to pay for a full day. Hmm! At the exit barrier, I made a display of searching the car and my wallet and, eventually, smiling sheepishly up at the bloke in the kiosk, said, 'I can't find my ticket.'

'In that case,' came the smug reply from Mr. Jobsworth, 'I will have to charge you for a full day's parking. It's the rules, and it says so on the sign.'

'That's OK, mate,' I replied, handing him a tenner instead of the best part of forty pounds. 'It's my fault for losing the ticket. You're only doing your job.'

I was still sniggering about my victory as we drove off Gibraltar and into Spain. Kim thinks I'm easily amused by such things, but in this day and age, I see such matters as major victories for we ordinary folk against the rules and regulations of an increasingly bureaucratic state. Saving thirty pounds was pretty good too.

Back to the present trip, though, and as Gibraltar receded into the mist, the road took us through San Roque, where we'd been just two months earlier to collect a car I'd just bought, and towards Estepona, which is where the touristy area starts and the Northern Europeans like to buy holiday homes or retire to play golf. Marbella, which a friend once described rather accurately, to my way of thinking, as "Essex-by-the-Sea", is a little further along this stretch of coast. We weren't going as far as this, and at San Pedro de Alicante, we turned away from the coast to head up the mountain road towards Ronda, which is where we were about to have our rather scary "incident".

Ronda is 750 metres (2,460 feet) higher than the coast, and the 44-km (27-mile) route is along a road that's almost like an alpine pass — lots of tight bends linked together by short straights. The type of road that bikers seek just for the sheer pleasure of riding them. I'd ridden this route a few times before, and I'd deliberately chosen Ronda as our overnight destination so that I could have another go at it. As we climbed higher, we were ascending into the clouds, and although it wasn't raining, it was damp and foggy, and as the early evening approached, the temperature had become significantly cooler — cold, in fact.

The road was shiny with moisture which I realised would provide less traction than in dry conditions. The bike was fully laden, so whilst I was enjoying positioning the bike for the next bend, selecting the right gear, applying just the right pressure to the handlebars to induce the counter-steering that would lay the bike over to take the bend, I was very mindful that the conditions were less than ideal for this type of road. I thought I'd felt the tyres squirm a little on a couple of occasions, and that was fair warning to take things easy, so I wasn't by any means pushing things and certainly not trying to find any limits. I was enjoying myself, but cautiously.

I lay the bike over to take a right-hander, and as the turn tightened into a decreasing radius bend, which was something I was already anticipating on this road, the bike simply didn't take the line I'd selected and drifted over the white line into the opposite lane and towards a sheer drop on the far side. I felt powerless to pull her back, and I distinctly remember thinking that, if I lay her over any more, I would lose her. Eventually, the road straightened up, and I was able to re-cross the white line and regain my side of the road, thanking God, Allah, Krishna and Buddha that nothing had been coming in the opposite direction, otherwise, with no run-off area to speak of, it could very well have been goodnight from Kim and goodnight from Andy.

My heart was beating ten to the dozen as we gingerly made our way up the mountain at a much slower pace. A queue of cars soon formed behind us. *Bollocks to them*, I thought. *They have four wheels, and I only have two on what's proved to be a slippery road surface, so they can follow at my pace.* Kim leaned forward and asked what had just happened. I shrugged to indicate I had no idea and gave her knee what I hoped was a reassuring pat. My main goal now was to get us both up the mountain and arrive at our hotel in one piece, however long it took.

We eventually arrived, shaken and stirred, in Ronda, where because we'd previously stayed at our ultimate destination, we lost no time in finding the Hotel Catalonia.

Whilst Kim went to check us in, I managed to light a ciggie and calm down a little before unloading the bike, dumping the luggage in reception and parking Roadie in the adjacent car park. Kim asked me again what had happened on the mountain. 'I honestly don't know,' I replied. 'I just thought that, if I lay the bike down any more, I would lose it, and that's why we ended up on the wrong side of the road. I'm not sure if the bike slid, or if I just got it totally wrong.'

'I thought I felt it sliding,' Kim observed.

Hmm, I thought, *sliding or not, it was still my fault. We could have had a serious accident there, and I should never have put us in such a situation.*

'Well, whatever caused it, I need a drink.'

So, stripping off our wets and leaving them in reception with the luggage, we headed to the bar for something to calm our nerves.

Later, having changed out of our riding gear in our very comfortable and well-appointed room, we went down to the hotel restaurant for dinner. On entering the bar, I spotted they had a selection of "gourmet" beers on offer, one of which was Newcastle Brown Ale. I'm not sure whether the average Geordie would regard "Broon Ale" as being part of a fine dining experience, but I have to say that a few bottles of Newcastle's finest went down very well that evening. It had been a long day following a late night, so we were in bed by 10 p.m.

So, that was the end of Day One. A total of 506 kilometres (314 miles) travelled, seven and a half hours on the road, one Furthest Point ticked off and at least one pair of very soiled underpants. If the rest of the trip was going to be anything like Day One, it would prove to be an interesting experience, to say the least, not to mention possibly our last.

Isla de Las Palomas, the Furthest Point South

5

Day 2, 8 May

Route: Ronda
Distance today: 0 kilometres (0 miles)
Distance so far: 506 kilometres (324 miles)
Bike time: None
Overnight: Hotel Catalonia, Ronda

We awoke at 10 a.m., having slept the clock around. I looked through the curtains to see that the rain was bucketing down. Good weather for ducks, perhaps, but not very good for bikers. Fortunately, we weren't intending to do any biking that day because we were booked in for two nights at the Hotel Catalonia. As if in sympathy with the grim weather, I was feeling pretty grim myself. I'd been trying to fight the onset of a cold for a few days and had been hoping it would just go away. During the night, however, the sneaky cold germs had taken hold, and it had arrived in full force. As any man knows, the symptoms of a cold are debilitating. Why women don't appreciate this is quite beyond me. If women were to take just a moment to pause for thought in the last stages of childbirth, just before the head makes an appearance, for example, they would understand what it's like to be a man with a cold. Anyway, I'm not trying for sympathy here, so let's just say I was feeling totally crappy.

By the time we'd got showered and dressed, it was too late to have breakfast in the hotel, so we strolled the short distance to the main plaza in downtown Ronda. We soon found a café and got on the outside of some good coffee and delicious ham and cheese toasties. As we sat, several tour groups, mainly consisting of either old people, Chinese people or old Chinese people dressed in plastic ponchos, rain hats and carrying umbrellas, wandered round the plaza looking damp and miserable in the rain, which was still bucketing down. The tour groups followed tour guides who carried flags on the tops of long poles. What exactly is that all about? Are grown-up people incapable of following a tour guide without the guide having to carry an identification flag? It seems not.

I also suppose that the tour groups were a little disappointed because, being Sunday, almost all the shops were closed except one selling plastic ponchos, rain hats and umbrellas, and the owner was doing a roaring trade. He probably decided to open on Sunday just because of the weather, and if so, I had to admire such an entrepreneurial spirit.

Ronda is situated atop huge cliffs and is a lovely little town. Its history goes back to several centuries before Christ, probably because of its strategic and easily defendable position. The Romans settled here, and it was an important city and the capital of the region during the time that the Moors ruled Spain. Today it retains much of its old charm, and a lot of Islamic architecture still remains.

The town is bisected by the El Tajo Gorge which carries the Guadalevín River some 100 metres (320 feet) below. In the 18th century, the locals were beginning to find it inconvenient to use the two old bridges to cross from one side of the town to the other because crossing entailed a steep climb down one side of the gorge and another equally steep climb at the other side. Therefore, in 1735, a new bridge was commissioned by King Felipe V to span the gorge at city level. An architect was appointed to design the bridge, but it collapsed after only six years with the loss of around fifty lives. This gives credence to the well-known fact in construction circles that, if you want a bridge designing properly, go to a structural engineer and not to an architect.

The second attempt proved to be more successful, and although it took forty-two years to complete, the Puento Nuevo is still standing and in use by both modern traffic and tourists who seem intent on risking life and limb to take photos from impossible angles. The bridge has also had some other uses, not all related to public transportation. There's a chamber under the central arch that has been used, amongst other things, as a gaol and a bar, although not at the same time. Criminals were sometimes thrown off the bridge, and rumour has it that Hemingway's description in *For Whom the Bell Tolls* of the execution of Nationalist sympathisers in the Spanish Civil War by being thrown from cliffs is based on killings that took place at the cliffs of El Tajo.

Ronda is also the birthplace of modern bullfighting and the Plaza de Toros de Ronda is the oldest bullfighting ring in Spain and is well worth a visit, not to see any bulls being killed, of course, but to have a mooch round the fine museum. Before bullfighting as we know it today, the bulls were killed by horsemen using spears. Pedro Romero, however, thought the odds were unfairly weighted against the bull and came up with the novel idea of dispensing with the horse and using a cape and a sword especially designed for the kill. In some eyes, Pedro transformed bullfighting into an art and a skill in its own right and not simply a preamble to the bull's slaughter. Having said that, Pedro personally killed 285 bulls in 1776 alone and lived to the grand old age of eighty-five, so it's difficult to see how the odds were stacked very favourably towards the bulls.

Ronda also possesses a rather fine museum. I'm not sure it's a museum in the traditional sense because it's more like a private collection of stuff that is open to the public for an admission fee. Whatever it is, it's well worth the admission price, and I had, on a previous visit, spent an interesting couple of hours wandering round and looking at various seemingly unrelated collections of artefacts. A collection of photographic equipment would lead on to a collection of household utensils, medical instruments or some such. It was as though the collector had just indulged in his or her passion for collecting and then decided to put everything on display to the public. Most of the displays weren't under glass or protected in any way, and there was little attempt to explain anything, which made it a pleasing change from formal museums where the feeling is that you're there to be educated rather than just to enjoy looking at the items on display.

In the basement, there was a collection of instruments of torture used by the Spanish Inquisition. There were also a few illustrations of the various implements in use, and a chill ran up my spine at the thought that the very things I was looking at could have been used to cause terrible suffering to ordinary people just like myself.

The Spanish Inquisition, as well as being made famous by *Monty Python's Flying Circus*, was an organisation whose purpose in life was to discover heretics and then to punish them for, well, being heretics, I suppose. The usual punishment was to be burned at the stake, but if those who were found guilty repented and denounced their heretical religion, their sentence would be reduced so that they would just be garrotted before being set on fire. Not all bad then!

The history of the Spanish Inquisition is interesting, and to understand it we must go back to the first century AD, which is when the Moors came from North Africa and, within quite a short period, occupied the whole of the Iberian Peninsula. The border between Christian and Islamic Spain shifted constantly over the centuries, but southern Spain, and particularly Andalucía, remained firmly in control of the Moors until the late fifteenth century when the combined forces of Spain, led by King Ferdinand and his wife, Queen Isabella, finally regained control. In an attempt to consolidate the newly united Spain, Jews (who formed a sizeable proportion of the population) and those who practised Islam were given a choice — either renounce your faith and convert to Catholicism or leave your land, your property, all your money and possessions behind and bugger off. It's not recorded, but it's probable that this edict also extended to Methodists, Seventh Day Adventists, Baptists, Druids and anyone who wasn't a Catholic.

Not surprisingly, a sizeable number opted for conversion rather than the unpleasant alternative of poverty and exile from the land where they'd lived for many generations. The Jewish converts were known as the converted and the Moorish converts as little Moors. The converts, however, faced continual suspicion and prejudice and many who'd professed conversion continued to practise their faith in secret. This was deemed to be subversive, and the Spanish Inquisition was tasked with seeking out such heretics who were considered to be a danger to the existence of Christian Spain. The Inquisition would turn up in a town with a cunning plan for seeking out heretics. This consisted of asking people to denounce any suspects. The accused would be rounded up, tortured until they confessed and then executed.

The Inquisitors were forbidden from drawing blood when extracting confessions; obviously, this was considered as being a bit too barbaric, but it didn't stop them from devising some pretty horrendous, bloodless alternatives. One of the machines I saw in the museum consisted of a stout chair in which the accused would be strapped down. A metal cone in the centre of the seat was attached to a winch mechanism which gradually raised the cone into the victim's anus. I would have probably admitted to being anything they wanted me to admit to before even being strapped down.

There was a bit of a flaw in this system — not the chair, but the system of finding potential heretics. If you fancied your boss' job or your neighbour's wife, or if some bloke had just annoyed you by blocking your driveway with his carriage or letting his dog shit on your lawn, you could simply denounce him to the Inquisition and from thenceforth enjoy an increased salary, a bit on the side, an unobstructed drive or a clean lawn.

Anyway, we'd done the bridge, the bullring, the museum and several other things on previous trips. This time we were here to do a bit of hiking and explore the gorge. There were only two problems — it was still bucketing down, and my flu was rapidly turning into a full-on viral infection. As expected, I received absolutely no sympathy from my beloved who declared she wasn't going to be put off by a bit of rain when there was a perfectly good canyon to be hiked, so we decided on a compromise. Kim would go for a hike, and I would return my fevered body to the hotel and take it easy. We departed the café, and Kim set off in the direction of the gorge whilst I, in severe danger of having an eye put out from several umbrellas brandished by old people / Chinese people / old Chinese people which, by virtue of their short stature, resulted in the pointy bits of the umbrellas being exactly at my eye level, made my way across the plaza and up the hill towards the hotel. By the way, the Spanish for umbrella is *paraguas*, literally "for water", which I think is rather charming.

I was puffing and panting when I arrived at the hotel. Maybe it wasn't a virus after all but the onset of pneumonia?

Kim arrived back a couple of hours later, full of smiles and most enthusiastic about her walk. She'd descended the gorge and walked its length, getting soaked through during the process. After a spot of lunch together, she took herself off to the hotel gym and spa, whilst I returned to the room to lie on the bed and moan quietly to myself.

The thought of yesterday's "oops, nasty" on the mountain road was still very much in my mind. I still had difficulty understanding what had happened or why I'd essentially not been able to control the bike. I'd obviously had a few hairy moments whilst biking. What biker hasn't if they've ridden a lot of miles? My previous escapades, however, had invariably been a result of other road users and a lack of concentration on my part, rather than my bike-handling skills. When I lived in Dubai, I used to teach safe-rider skills to both new and experienced riders, for God's sake!

So why did the bike drift over the white line? Yes, the road was wet and would have had reduced traction, but I still didn't think I was overdoing things. Did the bike slide as Kim thought it had? It would be unusual for both tyres to slide at the same time and rate; usually either the front or rear will let go, and it certainly didn't feel as if that had happened. The tyres were reasonably new, had plenty of tread, weren't approaching their sell-by date, and I'd checked the pressures the day before we set off, so I doubted they were the cause of the problem.

I started to think about accident statistics. In the majority of bike-related accidents where there was no other vehicle involved, investigations put the reason down to rider error rather than the capabilities of the bike. In other words, the bike would have made it had the rider not messed things up. I'd got myself out of a few hairy situations, such as entering a corner at a speed that my brain suddenly decided was a bit too quick, by using the mantra "trust the bike" to stop me bottling it and doing something stupid and compounding the situation.

In his excellent book *A Twist of the Wrist II*, Keith Code, former motorcycle racer, writer and founder of the California Superbike School, talks about "survival reactions". These are deeply embedded in all of us when faced with a potentially dangerous situation and are otherwise known as the "fight or flight" syndrome. On a motorcycle, these translate into rolling off the gas, tightening of the grip on the handlebars, narrowing our field of view, fixing attention on something, steering in the direction of the fixed attention, freezing instead of steering, or ineffective steering and braking in an inappropriate time and place. Unfortunately, most of these are BAD things to do when riding a motorcycle.

A motorcycle's weight distribution is around 50% to each tyre, so if we roll off the gas or, even worse, brake whilst cornering, this will transfer the weight from rear to front and may overload the front tyre which may consequently lose traction. The correct way is to either maintain a constant throttle whilst the bike is cranked over, or to gradually apply the gas.

Holding onto the bars too tightly stops the bike from doing what it's designed to do, which is to self-correct for road imperfections and steer in a constant line. It results in the bike running wide in turns because we're unconsciously counter-steering it to the outside. The message here is to relax arms and wrists at all times and let the bike do what it's supposed to do.

Narrowing our field of view and target fixation means our brains are concentrating on the danger and not on how to get out of the danger. A car pulls out of a T-junction in a classic SMIDSE (sorry, mate, I didn't see you) situation. Our instinct is to fix all our attention on the car, whereas we should be fixing our attention on the escape route we need to take, or the stopping point we need to achieve to avoid hitting the car. Allied to this situation is the fact that the bike will go wherever we're looking, so if we're looking at the car because it's become a hazard, there's a good chance we'll hit it. We should be looking at the part of the road we need to be on to miss the car.

Putting this into practice in yesterday's situation meant that, when the bike started to drift towards the white line, what I should have done was to keep a steady throttle, maintain a relaxed hold on the bars whilst pushing the right-hand bar a little to tighten the turn and to look inside the corner towards where I wanted to be. Did I do this? I honestly don't know. All I can say is that, knowing what you *should* do is one thing but putting it into practice when your brain is shouting, 'YOU ARE ABOUT TO DIE,' is sometimes another thing entirely. With these thoughts running through my mind, I dropped off into a siesta until Kim returned.

In the evening, dinner was to be in the town, where we found Nonno Pepe, a friendly little Italian restaurant where the pizzas and wine were superb. This isn't going to be the type of book in which the writer assumes the reader needs to know exactly what each of us consumed during each meal and exactly what it cost. Let me just say, however, that €28 for two excellent pizzas and a bottle of red in a very touristy town wasn't bad at all.

Dinner was followed by a stroll back up the hill, a nightcap in the hotel, and we were in bed by ten thirty, hoping the weather would improve for tomorrow when we needed to be back on the road.

Puento Nuevo, Ronda

6

Day 3, 9 May

Route: Ronda — Campillos — Granada — Guadix — Lorca
Distance today: 408 kilometres (254 miles)
Distance so far: 914 kilometres (568 miles)
Bike time: 6 hours
Overnight: Parador de Lorca, Lorca

Monday morning dawned overcast, drizzly and grey, but the good news was that my bubonic plague had thankfully improved overnight. I was still feeling pretty snotty, but I was no longer feeling ill. As my old gran used to say, I was feeling "a lot better in meself".

We were up at eight thirty and were soon packed, ready for some breakfast and to hit the road. On reaching the dining room, however, we thought that €18 was a bit steep for breakfast, so we decided to settle for a couple of coffees and to get something to eat whilst on the road. You'll never find complimentary tea and coffee in Spanish hotels, and this is because the Spanish like proper coffee made from coffee beans and would throw a fit at being offered the instant rubbish that comes in those sachets you can never open. My mom wouldn't like this situation — she likes to fill her handbag with all the free stuff she finds in hotel rooms and is probably the reason why hotels limit their pathetic offerings to just two of everything per day.

After persuading the staff to let us just have coffee, which proved to be a bit of a challenge, not because of the staff's unwillingness to serve us — in fact, they were very helpful — but because "the system" had seemingly made the executive decision that the only two options were a full breakfast or nothing and didn't allow them to enter "just coffee" into the computerised till. Systems often seem to be designed just to annoy the hell out of me and make life difficult.

Coffee and cigarettes consumed, I was feeling in a better frame of mind, and after loading the bike, programming Satnav Woman with our first way-point, we mounted Roadie at 9 a.m. and sallied forth for our next day of riding. The route took us through the countryside on B-roads towards Campillos, where we would eventually join an A-road to link up with the main route between Seville and Granada. It was cold on the road, and even though I was bundled up in all my layers and fairly comfortable, I had a distinctly numb forehead from the icy air. The traffic was light to non-existent, so I was enjoying the roads and the ride despite the cold and the damp.

We were on quiet roads, so it was about an hour before we found a likely-looking spot for breakfast at a gas station. Spain embraces the café culture, and it's perfectly normal to find cafés and restaurants situated next to, or forming part of, gas stations, especially in the rural areas. These are usually privately run enterprises that serve excellent fresh food and good coffee. This is in stark contrast to the UK's idea of roadside hospitality where motorway service stations offer pre-packaged, expensive rubbish, and road-side vans sell cholesterol rolls served with instant coffee in a paper or polystyrene cup.

We were sitting in the comfortably warm café with our usual coffees and toasties when a smartly dressed guy strolled over for a chat.

'*Hola. ¿Esa es su Harley?*' (Hello. Is that your Harley?)

'*Hola, Señor. Sí, es nuestra moto.*' I replied that, yes, it was our motorcycle, thinking that, as we were the only other customers and were dressed in full biking gear, it was a bit of a daft question.

'*También tengo una Harley.*' (I also have a Harley.)

'*Ah, hermano. Muy bien. ¿Que tipo tienes?*' (Nice one, mate. What d'you ride?)

There followed a typical biker conversation between two total strangers, one of whom had pretty limited language skills in the other's mother tongue. We managed to exchange views on bikes in general, Harleys in particular, roads, routes and other general biking stuff. I like this about the biking community; it's a bit like being part of a brotherhood who all look out for, and help, one another. There are exceptions, of course, but in general, if you're stuck at the side of the road with your bike, it will be another biker who stops to offer assistance.

After fifteen minutes or so practising my Spanish with my new friend, it was time to saddle up and head on down the road. It was raining steadily, but thankfully, the rain stopped after about thirty minutes, and whilst the skies were still leaden, at least it was dry.

The road swept us through the Parque de Gualdaltepe with mountains on one side and an aqua-coloured lake on the other. Stunningly gorgeous. The fields were white and appeared to be covered in frost, but they were, in fact, tiny white wildflowers. Kim later said she thought it may have been thyme. I asked where the parsley, sage and rosemary had been, but Kim, not being a Simon and Garfunkel fan, sadly missed the joke.

After 90 or so kilometres (55 miles) of sparsely trafficked A- and B-roads, we connected with the A-92 DC, a dual carriageway carrying the traffic from Seville towards Granada; Granada being the direction in which we were heading. The traffic was quite light at first but became heavier as we approached Granada. It was on the outskirts that, having so far covered about 800 kilometres (500 miles) on our trip, we encountered our first dickhead. I was in the outside lane, steadily overtaking what was pretty much nose-to-tail traffic, when Mr Golf GTi Driver planted himself about half a metre behind

Roadie's rear mudguard and started flashing his headlights. I have no idea where he thought I could move to to let him pass. Cars were closely spaced on the inside lane, and I was travelling quite a bit faster than them, anyway. There was a car in front of me, so I couldn't speed up. Maybe I should have ordered a helicopter with a skyhook to lift me off the road to allow him to pass beneath me. I was eventually able to find a space in the inside lane into which I could safely pull to let him pass. Then I turned to give him my steely biker glare as he shot past. He stared fixedly ahead and continued acting like a dickhead with the next guy in front.

This type of driving behaviour is very rare in Spain and, whilst many Brits complain about what they consider to be poor standards of driving there, they probably haven't lived in Africa or the Middle East. Having lived in both locations, I consider Spanish drivers in general to be both courteous and of a pretty good standard. It's all relative, I suppose. Sure, you do sometimes get dozy old blokes who pootle along without a care in the world, seemingly totally unaware of other road users. When I last lived in the UK, such people were usually driving an Austin Allegro, wearing a trilby hat and smoking a pipe. I'm sure that the more modern equivalent still exists.

As we bypassed Granada, the sun made an appearance for the first time on our trip. It was very welcome, but unfortunately, it didn't last for long, and as Granada receded in Roadie's mirrors, the rain made a reappearance. This was a bit of a bummer because I'd previously enjoyed a great drive in our BMW along this road, which winds its way through the forested foothills of the Sierra Nevada, and I was looking forward to repeating the experience on the bike. The road is a dual carriageway, but its twists and turns through lovely countryside give it more the feeling of an A-road. My last trip had been in December when the traffic was light and driving conditions were perfect, so a bit of spirited driving had been called for. The BMW's three-litre, six-cylinder engine and sports suspension meant we were soon pushing along, as solid as a rock between 160 and 190 kph (100 and 120 mph), and I had a great time.

This time, however, the rain had intensified, and we were soon riding on wet roads. The spray from other vehicles, combined with the heavy rain, provided limited visibility. Such conditions meant I wouldn't be repeating the experience on the Harley today, and the incident on the mountain road to Ronda was still unsettling me, so we made our way at an appropriately sensible speed for the conditions.

The road eventually climbs to a plateau at 1,350 metres (4,430 feet) above sea level. The rain had stopped by the time we reached it, and looking all round us, we couldn't see anything higher in elevation. It felt as though we were on top of the world. The sun made another brief reappearance, but the road was heading towards some ominous-looking black clouds, so we were expecting the worst. We felt a few heavy drops of rain, but the road suddenly veered off in another direction, and we bypassed the cloud. Yay! Don't you love it when stuff like that happens? It's like putting on a pair of jeans you haven't worn for a while and finding a fiver in the pocket.

The road heads towards Guadix, past huge, red-coloured bluffs that reminded me of a time when we rode through parts of Arizona. The main difference between here and Arizona was that it was hot and sunny in Arizona, and it was cold, wet and miserable on the road to Guadix.

As we approached, we soon started to see some of the cave houses for which this area is famous. The rock here contains many natural caves and is also easily carved out, so for many centuries, the local population have used this to their advantage and converted the natural caves into dwellings. The cave houses often have shallow, man-made facades, just like conventional houses, but the main part of the houses are contained within warrens of underground rooms with rock-cut windows peeking out of cliffs and chimneys poking out of grassy roofs. Today, the cave houses range from small, holiday-type cottages to top-of-the-range caves with swimming pools, underfloor heating and spa baths, so there is something for every hobbit, whatever the depth of his pocket.

Leaving Guadix after a stop for gas and lunch, the landscape became very barren, just sand-coloured hills with isolated bushes, and was quite reminiscent of both the Middle East and some of the western regions in the United States. This isn't at all surprising because the Tabernas Desert is the driest region in Europe and has the continent's only true desert climate. This fact seemed totally bizarre, considering we'd just ridden through the green and verdant forests bordering the Sierra Nevada and the fact it had been belting it down with rain for most of today's ride. The similarity between this area and the Wild West was the reason it was used in the 1960s to film a number of Spaghetti Westerns of the type made famous by producer Sergio Leone and starring Clint Eastwood. Several movies have been filmed here since then.

You can visit Fort Bravo, Oasys Theme Park and Eastern Leone where "Western" towns still contain the sets from numerous movies and have now turned into tourist attractions. These are still used for filming, and if you visit them, you'll be walking in the footsteps of celebrities and actors such as Clint Eastwood, Brigitte Bardot, Anthony Quinn, Claudia Cardinale, Sean Connery, Raquel Welch, Orson Wells and many more. We didn't stop for a visit, but in my mind's eye, looking over the landscape as we rode our modern version of the outlaw's horse, I could see a group of cowboys and a stagecoach being chased by Indians into one of the arroyos, where, no doubt, the US cavalry would come to their rescue just in time. Looking in another direction, I think I saw a cowboy, dressed in a wide-brimmed hat and wearing a poncho, take his cigar out of the corner of his mouth and spit tobacco juice on his lady companion's dog. You just gotta love Clint!

As we pushed on, the wind became strong and gusty. My least favourite weather for riding a bike is wind. Rain is OK if you're suitably protected. Cold and heat may be controlled by dressing suitably, but there is nothing you can do about windy conditions. If you're riding into the wind, it increases the noise in your helmet, and the increased airflow makes it feel as if you're going faster than you are. The opposite is true if you have a following wind, and if the wind is coming from the side or quarter, you can lean into it to counteract its force on the bike. When overtaking trucks, you get used to the bow wave of air which appears just as you're passing the front of the truck. This, however, tends to affect lighter bikes more than heavier ones such as Roadie. When the direction of the wind causes you to be in the lee of the truck whilst overtaking, however, the bow wave effect is increased as you leave the shelter of the truck and the wind hits you again. Even Roadie gets buffeted off course in these conditions, but I've learned to anticipate it and, therefore, correct for it instantly.

It's not so bad if the wind is steady and from a consistent direction, but that day it was very gusty, and because you can't see the gusts coming, you can't anticipate them. The gusts constantly pushed Roadie off course, and I continually had to straighten her back on track. You can't see a gust of wind coming, of course, so the first thing you know about it is when it hits you. It pushes the bike off course as it hits your body and the bike. It causes a sudden noise in your ears as it buffets your helmet and tries to knock your head off your shoulders. Consequently, each time a gust hits you, your brain panics, and this causes your body to go into survival-reaction mode and tense up, ready to fight or fly. Riding tensely stops the bike doing what it's supposed to do, which is to self-correct the steering. The trick is to ride loose and relaxed and let the bike do the work. Convincing your frequently panicking brain of this, however, is something that's much easier said than done, and riding in these conditions is not only extremely unpleasant but very tiring.

Our destination for the night was to be Lorca, where we'd booked into the appropriately named Parador de Lorca. Paradors and their Portuguese equivalents, pousadas, are a great invention because they not only help to preserve historic buildings that otherwise may have slipped into rack and ruin but enable you to stay in them. They were created by the Spanish and Portuguese governments to use the income created from the accommodation to contribute to the upkeep of the buildings and to contribute to the local economy. If you choose to stay in a parador, you could find yourself bedding down in a castle, a palace, a convent, a monastery, a fortress or a variety of other historic buildings.

Parador de Lorca is situated in an ancient castle. The thing about ancient castles, is that they were built with defence in mind and, consequently, they tend to be located in easily defensible locations with good views over the surrounding countryside. This inevitably means on the top of a very high hill. They're often surrounded by equally ancient buildings and streets that were built with horses and donkeys in mind rather than cars and motorcycles.

Satnav Woman had been programmed to guide us to our destination, and this she did by choosing the most direct route which took us up slippery, cobbled streets with tight corners and hairpin bends on very steep gradients. Just the type of thing you need when you're riding a big motorcycle two-up and carrying three weeks' worth of luggage. When we left the parador the next day, I followed a lovely, modern, tarmac road that led us back into Lorca centre and then onto our new route. I also noticed some handy signs directing weary travellers to the parador. Satnav Woman strikes again!

Having previously stayed in a couple of castles, a former convent, a former hospital and a former monastery, we were disappointed to find that Lorca's parador was a modern hotel. Granted, it was set within the castle walls and had been cleverly built so as to display some ancient foundations. Whilst we were impressed by its quality, and I liked the modern design, it just wasn't the ancient building we'd been expecting.

After unloading the bike and checking in at 3:30 p.m., we dropped our bags and riding gear in our well-appointed room and set off downstairs for a late lunch. Our waiter looked as though he was from the days of the original castle. He had a distinct similarity to the manservant from *Young Frankenstein* and carried his tray like Julie Walters in Victoria Wood's *Two Soups* sketch. We noticed later that he'd abandoned the tray and was using a trolley to serve the customers. This probably ensured that most of the food and drink arrived on the plates and in the glasses, rather than on the tray.

After a bit of a snooze, we spent half an hour exploring the grounds and castle walls which overlook Lorca far below and far beyond into the distance. By eight o'clock, the day was ending in a beautiful evening, with no wind and clear, blue skies. It was a shame it hadn't been like this all day.

We enjoyed a leisurely dinner in the parador, washed down with several glasses of red, and retired at a quarter to midnight.

At the end of our second riding day, we'd covered 914 kilometres (568 miles), which is about the same distance as London to Inverness and almost the same as London to Zurich. We'd also seen the sun twice during the day.

Kim not showing her helmet hair

Day 4, 10 May

Route: Lorca — Denia
Distance today: 256 kilometres (159 miles)
Distance so far: 1,170 kilometres (727 miles)
Bike Time: 3 hours 45 minutes
Overnight: Yasmin and David's, Denia

Day four of our trip dawned, well, pretty much the same as days one, two and three — raining, with not a break in the overcast skies. I checked the weather forecast and cheered up a little when I found that, whilst there would be rain in Lorca, it would be dry in Denia, which was to be that day's destination, so hopefully, we should ride out of the rain before too long.

We were up at nine o'clock, and after a couple of cups of coffee, we were checked out, loaded up, clad in our waterproofs and ready to sally forth by ten fifteen. As we rode, the forecast proved to be correct, and the rain began to relent, but it still remained cloudy and grey with occasional short periods of rain. We were following Satnav Woman's "fastest route", so after breakfast at the far side of Murcia, we found ourselves riding along the dual carriageway between Murcia and Alicante.

Murcia is Spain's seventh largest city with a population of 473,000, and Alicante is the ninth largest with 335,000, so this is a well-travelled route, and the traffic was quite heavy with a lot of trucks and commercial vehicles. The weather, the traffic and the drab landscape resulted in this not being the most enjoyable of rides, and if we hadn't been trying to make good time, I would have looked for an alternative route.

This type of traffic situation, whilst not unusual in Spain, is not as common as it is in the UK. True, round major cities, the traffic does get dense, but there are vast areas in Spain and Portugal where the roads are very quiet, which makes driving or riding such a pleasure. Doing the same thing the in the UK, for me at least, has largely become something of an unenjoyable chore these days. There's a very good reason for this. Whilst the UK has some 419,000 kilometres (260,000 miles) of roads on which they've managed to squeeze 38 million vehicles, Spain has just 33 million vehicles to share 666,000 kilometres (413,000 miles) of roads. In other words, the UK has 91 vehicles per kilometre of road (146 per mile), but Spain only has 48 (80 per mile), or almost half the traffic density.

Another splendid thing about driving or riding in Spain is the absence of traffic cones. Obviously, the road systems need to be maintained and upgraded, but when the Spanish do this, those responsible seem to do it quickly and return the road to normal as soon as possible. Why is it that when I'm crawling at 80 kph (50 mph) for mile upon mile on the M1 in the UK, no one ever seems to be working on the roadworks that have caused the problem? I've worked in construction for my entire career, and I've worked on projects in the Middle East where thirty-storey buildings have been completed in less time than it takes contractors in the UK to lay a bit of new tarmac between Sheffield and Rotherham. It beggars belief.

So, back to the trip. We'd deliberately planned a short ride that day so that we could maximise our time with our friends Yasmin and David (a.k.a. Yaz and Dava) with whom we would be staying for the next two days. Whilst this route wasn't exactly the best for an enjoyable ride, it would enable us to be with them in Denia by early afternoon.

Alicante's ring-road system eventually spat us out onto the road that heads north-east along the coast towards our destination. Leaving Alicante behind, the traffic gradually thinned, and the ride became much more enjoyable with glimpses of the Mediterranean as the route swooped and curved over the hilly terrain.

About forty minutes later, Benidorm, the city that's so beloved of UK package tourists, hove into view on our right. I was amazed to see a couple of very tall tower buildings that hadn't been there when I was last in the area. Having lived and worked in the Middle East for about twenty years, I was used to seeing, and even working on, pretty high buildings, but to see the twin, fifty-two-storey towers of the Intempo building on the Spanish coast was a shock. Work began on the Intempo in 2007, and it was eventually completed seven years later. This is more than twice the time a similar project would take in Dubai, but hey, credit due to the Spanish builders, because this is the tallest residential building in Spain. Why anyone would want to live in Benidorm is quite frankly beyond me, but I guess we all have different perceptions of what's good in life. Maybe the average Benidorm resident would find the area where we live somewhat lacking in full English breakfasts, John Smiths beer and nightly premiership football and feel it to be a bit boring, but each to their own.

The only time I'd visited Benidorm was eleven years earlier, and this wasn't through personal choice. At the time, we were living in Abu Dhabi, and I was the assistant director of the Abu Dhabi Harley Owners Group (HOG) Chapter. HOG is something peculiar to Harley-Davidson and is a brilliant piece of marketing by the company. Each Harley-Davidson dealership has an associated chapter which is run on fairly strict guidelines set down by HOG and, I guess ultimately, by Harley-Davidson itself. The HOG motto is "To Ride and Have Fun", which is a great objective and something I wholeheartedly agree with. However, because the chapter officers are all volunteers who offer up their services for different reasons, and organisations staffed by volunteers being what they are, it sometimes ends up being more like "To Ride a Bit and Have Politics". Nevertheless, Kim and I have been members of chapters in Bahrain, Abu Dhabi, Dubai and, more recently, the Algarve, and for the most part, these have meant we've met a lot of good people, ridden a lot of miles in agreeable company and had many hours of, well, riding and having fun, which is what it's supposed to be all about.

HOG organise yearly training camps for officers, and when I was with the Abu Dhabi Chapter, they offered to sponsor me to attend that year's event which was in — you've probably guessed — Benidorm. As the dealership and chapter between them would be paying for me to attend the two days of training, together with my flight and hotel costs, I jumped at the chance. In fact, I decided I would extend the two days into a week-long trip and take the opportunity to explore a bit of Spain whilst I was there.

I did a little research and soon worked out an itinerary that would involve me flying to Malaga, picking up a rental Harley in Marbella, spending two days on the road on the way to Benidorm, two days in Benidorm for the training and two days making my way back to Marbella before catching my flight home. This would be my first ever visit to Spain, a country I would eventually come to love and spend a significant amount of time in and which would become our home for a while.

After the long flight from Abu Dhabi, I landed in Malaga and grabbed a taxi to Marbella where I was staying the night before picking up the Harley the next day. It was evening by the time I'd checked in, so I went for a stroll with the intention of finding somewhere to have a couple of beers and dinner. I was lucky in my choice of hotel because it was right next to the old, traditional part of Marbella, and I soon found myself wandering through narrow streets into a plaza full of lively restaurants and bars. Taking an outside table, I relaxed with a cold beer and, for the first time, witnessed the *paseo*, which is another thing I've come to appreciate about Spain. The *paseo* is a traditional Spanish activity and is, in simple terms, the act of going for an evening stroll, either alone or with your spouse, partner, friends or family. In reality, it's not just a stroll but more of a social activity because this is the time of day when the Spanish meet up with their friends and family to talk about the day and catch up on news and gossip.

The kids also meet up and play, and the *paseo* often leads to coffee or tapas in one of the local cafés or restaurants. In my view, parents in the UK have become very overprotective of their children, and whether through necessity or not, they tend to keep them on a short leash. In Spain, however, it's usual for mom and dad, and probably grandma and grandad as well, to be enjoying a drink or snack in a café in the plaza, whilst close by, their kids play football, ride bikes, skateboard or just run round doing what kids do when they're having a good time with their pals. As I watched the lively activity surrounding me and soaked up the sounds of laughter emanating from people who were clearly enjoying themselves, I distinctly remember thinking I was witnessing a very agreeable way of life.

After an early night, I was up early the next day to meet Manolo who had a franchise for Eagle Rider motorcycle rentals and operated one of the few places in Spain where Harleys could be rented. Manolo soon introduced me to the black Heritage Softail that was to be my ride for the next six days. The Harley Softail range is designed for custom looks and has its rear suspension hidden under the frame to give the appearance of a hard-tail chopper that has no rear suspension at all. Although it looks cool, this setup doesn't do all that much for handling or for comfort on a long ride. The Heritage Softail is a bike designed for a classic 1950s look with a windscreen, leather panniers and spoked wheels and does look pretty cool, so if I had to choose one of the Softail models to go touring, this would definitely be the one.

Putting my wets and road map in the saddlebags, strapping my bag to the rear seat and cissy bar and waving goodbye to Manolo, I set out for my first ride on Spanish roads. I'd made a loose plan to follow the coast road out of Marbella, passing Malaga and Alicante en route to Benidorm, and that's pretty much what I did. Sometimes

I kept to the road as it hugged the coastline, and at others, I hopped on a motorway or ring road to avoid congested areas. It was a great ride, and I soon came to appreciate the Spanish road systems and lack of congestion in most of the areas I rode through. Bearing in mind what I said earlier about roadworks in Spain, at one point there was some new road construction going on where the tailbacks went on for many miles. This is where I learned something else that's good about riding in this region. Unlike the Middle East, where drivers never give way to anyone at all and will often deliberately obstruct others, the Spanish drivers are very biker-friendly and will move out of the way to let bikes pass. Consequently, I was able to ride the white line between stationary and slow-moving traffic and soon made short work of the queues. I'm still not sure what it is that makes Spanish motorists so actively friendly towards bikers. Maybe it's that many of them rode mopeds or scooters when they were young, or maybe it's just that, in general, the Spanish are helpful, friendly and polite people, but I like to believe they do things like this just because it's a nice thing to do.

I'd planned to spend two days on this part of my trip, but I made good progress, and despite coffee and cigarette breaks, the occasional gas stop and the roadworks, the 570 kilometres (350 miles) between Marbella and Benidorm were soon disappearing in my mirrors. I decided to press on to Benidorm, where I arrived in the early evening. Despite the fact I'd arrived a day earlier than my booking, I managed to check into the hotel where the HOG officer training was due to take place.

Dumping my bags in my room and changing out of my riding gear, I took a stroll round the great British institution that is Benidorm to find it was pretty much as I'd expected. It was very touristy and revealed very little to show me I was in Spain as opposed to a sunnier version of a seaside resort in Britain. It wasn't all bad, though because I treated myself to fish, chips and mushy peas washed down with a couple of pints of proper English beer before returning to the hotel for an early night. I know I said previously that, when living in Spain, these things had little appeal me, but at the time I was living in Abu Dhabi, so this was a rare treat.

Over breakfast on the hotel's agreeably sunny terrace and having a spare day before the training, I had a quick look at my map and decided to take a ride north along the coast with no particular destination in mind. I suppose it was the proximity to Benidorm that resulted in the coast road being quite busy, and my progress was a bit of a stop-start affair at first but became better as I put a bit of distance between myself and the resort.

After an hour or so, I found myself in Javia, where I parked up in the plaza so that I could have a coffee and sandwich in an adjacent café. A guy soon wandered up and sat at the next table.

'*¿Esa es su Harley?*' he asked and then, realising I wasn't Spanish, repeated his question in very good English. 'Is that your Harley?'

I explained it wasn't exactly mine but a rental. It turned out that my new friend was Dutch but had lived in Spain for most of his life. He was also a Harley rider and the local HOG director. He owned the estate agent's across the plaza, and we spent the next hour or so sipping coffee in the sun and talking bikes. When he realised I had no real plans for my ride, he insisted on paying my café bill, took me to his office, got out a map, photocopied a section and highlighted a circuitous route that would eventually take me back to Benidorm. This sort of thing is typical of the biker fraternity. It was doubtful we would ever meet again, but we'd spent an enjoyable hour in each other's company, and he'd gone out of his way to be helpful. I was later very happy that I followed his advice because the route took me deep into the Alicante countryside, through sleepy villages, along winding roads, over hills and down dales — a far cry from Benidorm. The weather was perfect, and his kindness resulted in me having a truly memorable day's ride.

When I returned to the hotel with a contented grin and a few flies on my face, the car park was pretty full of Harleys in all their various styles and guises. I spotted Spanish, Portuguese, Italian, French and a few other number plates, so it wasn't just me who'd decided to make the training course a good excuse for a ride.

After nipping up to my room to dump my riding gear and wash the dust off my face, I went down to the bar where, as I expected, the bikers had congregated to do what bikers enjoy second best after riding bikes i.e. drinking beer. A short while after being served a tall, cool one, two guys planted themselves in front of me. One was a barrel-chested guy with ponytail, mutton-chop sideburns and a big moustache, wearing an ancient riding vest adorned with hundreds of pins, patches and probably dead flies — the stereotypical Harley biker. His companion was about six foot two and looked only slightly less menacing.

'You're from Abu Dhabi then,' said Barrel-Chest in a rumbling, deep voice.

'Yes,' I replied a little cagily, realising they'd spotted my chapter patch and wondering whether they were a couple of Gulf War vets who had a grudge with the Middle East and its residents. Looking at the combined size of the two of them, I realised that, if they had bad intentions, it would probably end up being a pretty painful experience for me.

'Nice to meet you, mate,' rumbled Barrel-Chest, offering a meaty hand. 'I'm Kevin, and this is Mike. We're from the Dubai Chapter.'

Phew!

We spent the rest of the evening drinking beer, talking about bikes, chapter business and swapping tales about life in general. It turned out that both of them had, like me, spent many years working as expats. Kev was a Kiwi in the oil business who had lived and worked in many parts of the world including Nigeria, where I had my first experience as an expat. Mike was a civil engineer and had spent most of his career in the Middle East and had lived in Dubai for many years. It was a great night in good company. Little did I guess that, before a year had passed, circumstances would mean that Kim and I would move from Abu Dhabi to Dubai and Kev, Mike and our respective wives would all become riding buddies and good mates.

I don't remember much about the officer training of the next few days, but I do recall spending time with many good people from all over Europe, the Middle East and Africa, all of whom had the same wish to enjoy life and had a passion for biking in general and Harleys in particular. Some things do stand out, though.

The hotel was good and was one in which the more well-heeled visitors stay in Benidorm.

At breakfast one morning, the Italian HOG contingent started singing. I don't know if any of the posh residents complained, but the police were called. When they turned up, they simply smiled and said they couldn't arrest anyone for singing. It may have helped that one of the policemen was a bike cop.

At one point, I was sitting on the terrace enjoying a coffee and chatting to a husband and wife from Switzerland who were also there for the training. The wife told me they'd been into Benidorm centre earlier and had seen many drunken Brits wearing football shirts and generally behaving badly. As they were Swiss, behaving badly could have just meant that the people they'd seen were standing round in an untidily or unregulated manner.

'What exactly is this place?' she asked me.

Having been to Switzerland, I suspected this wouldn't be the sort of thing that would be acceptable, even to bikers in, say, Zurich or Geneva.

'It's a little piece of Britain that has been recreated on the Spanish coast, but to be honest, it's not a very good piece of Britain,' I advised her with a straight face.

I was able to catch up with my old friends Munther and Lisa whom I'd first met in Bahrain. Munther and his family owned the Harley-Davidson dealerships in Riyadh, Jeddah and Dammam in Saudi Arabia and, about a year after I'd obtained my first Harley, also opened up in Bahrain. Lisa was the general manager of the Bahrain dealership, and her daughter and son also worked for the business. Munther was a great bloke and became a Harley dealer, not because he thought it would be a profitable business, but because he was a biker and thought it would be a fun thing to do. Knowing Munther, I suspect it was a profitable business as well as being enjoyable for him. We'd all become good friends during my time in Bahrain, and it was great to see them again.

One night, many of the bikers ended up in a bar where a rock band was playing. Although the choice of music was good for a bunch of bikers, the band wasn't very good until a Swedish biker asked if he could do a few numbers with them. He turned out to be a really good guitarist and soon got the place rocking. I was tempted to offer my own vocal and guitar services, but realised that, whilst I could probably have held my own against the band, I was nowhere near as good as the Swedish guy so wisely decided to refrain from embarrassing myself.

Kev, Mike and I were out later when we spotted a group of people surrounding a car and taking photos of it. When we approached, we realised it was a Porsche Cayenne, but we couldn't understand what the fuss was about. It was only later we realised that, privileged that we were to live in the United Arab Emirates where cars such as this were about as commonplace as Volkswagen Golfs are in Europe, the people here had probably never seen one before.

After the two days' training, it was time to say goodbye to my new mates and everyone else I'd met, check out, saddle up and hit the road again. I'd decided to take a different route back to Marbella and to stop in Granada that night. I've no idea of the route I took. At each stop, I just looked at the map and decided which road looked good and would take me in the general direction of where I wanted to be. I love this type of trip.

After riding past the snow-capped Sierra Nevada mountains, I arrived in Granada during the late afternoon and found a likely-looking hotel whose receptionist said I was welcome to park the bike in their basement. What did I tell you about the Spanish having a good attitude to bikers? Dinner was at a restaurant, sitting at an outside table, but I soon beat a hasty retreat inside when the sun went down and the cold air descended from the mountains. It was freezing, especially after the warm, sunny day.

I had a similar experience the next morning when, although

sunny, it was distinctly chilly. Since leaving the UK in 1992, I'd lived in West Africa where the temperature is constantly around 30ºC (86ºF) and the Middle East where it's even hotter, sometimes reaching as much as 50ºC (122ºF), so I wasn't really used to cold weather anymore and had become, as my old gran used to say, "nesh". After about twenty minutes on the bike, I was shivering with cold. My fingers and toes were numb, and I felt chilled to the bone. Stopping at a gas station, I rummaged through my bag and donned just about every item of clothing I'd brought with me and topped everything off with my waterproofs. I looked like the Michelin Man, and the constriction of so many layers meant I could hardly get back on the bike. I didn't care, just so long as my frozen body regained some heat.

I made my way back to Marbella along various roads in pretty much the same manner as I'd arrived in Granada i.e. with no particular plan. My route took me to Ronda and down the very same mountain road that would later become the scene of the hairy moment I experienced with Kim. I arrived in Marbella in the late afternoon and somewhat reluctantly handed the Softail back to Manolo. My visit to Benidorm had been a truly memorable trip for so many reasons.

As Kim and I passed Benidorm on our current trip, we were only about an hour from Denia, and having visited Yasmin and David before, we were able to make our way straight to the marina where we'd agreed to meet them for lunch, arriving at around two o'clock. Yasmin looked her usual elegant self in dress, heels and designer sunglasses, and David carried off his Giorgio Armani look to a tee. Kim and I, on the other hand, looked like a couple of bikers that had just travelled 250 kilometres (155 miles) in wet weather. Such things don't matter one jot when you're with good friends, and after hugs, kisses and greetings, two slightly ill-matched couples were soon sitting at a table overlooking the yachts and boats and enjoying a long lunch.

The restaurant was in a prime position and was one of those places that, rather unusually for Spain, try to upsell everything and constantly encourage you to have extra this or that, which resulted in a hefty bill that was probably twice what we would expect to pay for something similar at home. This didn't spoil the occasion, however, even for two people from Yorkshire where we know the value of a pound. It was just great to be with our pals once again.

By five o'clock, we were sitting at the side of Yasmin and David's pool in the warm sunshine. Yes, that's correct — warm sunshine! During the afternoon, the clouds had receded, and the sun had made an appearance. This was the first time we'd experienced sun for more than a few moments on the trip, and this made it all the more enjoyable. In the evening, Yasmin cooked an excellent dinner, and we polished off a few bottles of wine whilst exchanging news and bringing each other up to date with what was happening in our lives. Fatigued by the ride and the red wine, I sensibly retired at around ten o'clock. I learned the next morning that Kim and Yasmin, despite being regularly in touch by phone, still managed to find enough to talk about until two in the morning. Judging by the empty bottles in evidence, however, they were more than likely talking utter rubbish.

Coffee stop on the road to Denia

8

Day 5, 11 May

Route: None
Distance today: None
Distance so far: 1,170 kilometres (727 miles)
Bike time: None
Overnight: Yasmin and David's, Denia

There was a nice surprise for me when I got up at nine o'clock — the sun was out, and it was a beautiful day in Denia. *About time*, I thought, whilst rummaging about in the bag for my shorts. 'Would you bloody believe it?' I muttered. 'We've been on the road for four days and travelled over a thousand kilometres, and the first nice day just happens to be when we aren't riding!'

'What are you chuntering about?' came an annoyed voice from the depths of the duvet.

'Nothing. D'you have any idea where my shorts are? The sun's out, and it might be my only chance to wear them on this trip.'

'Look on the shelf in the wardrobe where I put your things when I unpacked yesterday.'

Shorts duly found and donned, I wandered into the living area to find Yasmin, who, seeing me, uttered one of my favourite greetings. 'Morning. Would you like a sausage sandwich?' Stupid question. Yasmin knows there would only be one answer to that.

We first met Yasmin and David in Bahrain in the late nineties when Yasmin came to work for the company I was working for at the time. I was employed as a project manager on a pipeline project and was based on site, which meant I didn't get into the office very much, so it took a while for us to get to know each other. When the project was finished and I'd completed another job in Dubai, I found myself back in Bahrain working for the same company but, this time, working alongside Yasmin in the office. We soon got to know each other, found out that the same things made us laugh, and we quickly became good mates. I also came to realise that Yasmin and Kim shared many characteristics and tastes, so before long, I suggested we should go out as a foursome because I was sure Yasmin and Kim would get along famously.

My prediction proved to be an understatement, and the coming years would prove they were more like sisters who'd been separated at birth than just good friends. Their taste in everything from clothes to makeup, from handbags to sunglasses was so close they should have been able to negotiate discounts for bulk buying at their shops of preference. One year, Yasmin told me she couldn't think of anything to buy for Kim for Christmas, so I suggested she buy something she would really like for herself, and it would be fine. It was perfect. One year, they bought exactly the same things for each other.

Not everyone took to Yasmin immediately, however. Our daughter, Nina, who was a teenager at the time, had heard me talking about Yasmin and had heard me chatting to her on the phone and put two and two together and came up with seven or eight. The upshot of this was that, when Yasmin called at the house for the first time, Nina answered the door and, on Yasmin announcing who she was and asking for me, promptly closed the door in her face. The situation didn't last long, and Yasmin was, before long, giving Nina makeup tips and they were going shopping together. Nik, our son, who was also a teenager at the time, had no such inhibitions, and Yasmin once said she realised Nik felt at home at their place after he'd walked in and immediately checked their fridge for something to eat.

It's not always the case that, when two couples meet, everyone gets along with everyone else, but this was happily not the situation here, and a firm family friendship soon developed, a situation which happily still exists around twenty years later.

After David, Yasmin and I had munched our way through our sausage sandwiches and Kim had breakfasted on some yoghurt and berries or some other such healthy option, talk turned to plans for the rest of the day. I long ago learned that, when either Kim or Yasmin asks, 'What would you like to do?' the question is largely rhetorical because they'll either have their own ideas on the subject or will have previously decided what David and I would like to do. In such situations, I tend to keep my opinions to myself. Occasionally, rather than asking me such a question, Kim will proffer a suggestion from the outset along the lines of 'Shall we have a drive out to the Commercial Centre at Huelva for a lunch? You could pop into Leroy Merlin (Spain's equivalent of B&Q) to see if they have any new spanners.'

Ha! I know very well that in "Kim-speak" this actually means 'I would like to go for a mooch round Zara, Mango, Next and the other shops to see if they have anything I might like' and the suggestion of lunch and spanners is the only way she can get me to show any enthusiasm for such an expedition. Sometimes, however, she's a little subtler, so when, by some subterfuge or other, we've eventually got to an apparently random destination, the magic words "just" and "pop" will appear, as in 'Oooh! Whilst we're here, I might as well pop into IKEA because we need some new candles / pillow cases / wine glasses / whatever.' By my definition, the word "pop" means to go to a particular place for a short time. It doesn't mean spending the next two hours trolling round a shop, which seems to be Kim's definition, so I've come to dread those two little words.

Anyway, after David and I had informed the entertainment committee that we had no preference as to the day's activities, it was unanimously decided we would head into Denia and park up and have a stroll along the beach to a restaurant David and Yasmin had discovered. Depending on how long it took us to get there, we could either stay for coffee and a snack, or for lunch. The weather being beautiful, a walk on the beach was just the ticket as far as I was concerned, so we set off in their smart cabriolet down the mountain to Denia.

Denia is a likeable city of around 42,000 inhabitants and has a long and interesting history. It's been occupied since prehistoric times by such varied peoples as the Greeks, the Romans, the Moors and during the time of Napoleon, the French. The Moors built the castle that dominates the city, and the French rebuilt the castle that dominates the city, seemingly due to the shoddy workmanship of the Moorish builders. The city was reacquired by the Spanish in 1803, after which it became an important trading port. To add to this cosmopolitan mix, a community of English raisin traders lived in Denia from 1800 until the time of the Spanish Civil War in the 1930s, which just goes to show that today's expat British community in Denia isn't a particularly new phenomenon, although maybe these days, the Brits don't do so much trading in raisins. As well as being dominated by the castle, Denia is also dominated in a much bigger way by the Montgó mountain which forms a rocky peninsula between Denia and its southerly neighbour, Javia. David and Yasmin live on the northern slopes of the Montgó from where they enjoy spectacular views over the sea in one direction and the mountain's ridge in the other.

Today, Denia is a popular tourist destination, which is evidenced by the many holiday-home developments that stretch along its northern coast, and it possesses one of the most important harbours of the area, with a large fishing fleet and ferry connections to Ibiza.

The marina is extensive and offers the opportunity of a stroll or refreshment, and the town centre has an agreeable suburban feel and, as is usual in Spain, abounds with a variety of cafés, bars and restaurants.

Like me, David has spent his career in the construction industry, although on the design side rather than in construction, so as we walked along at the side of the beach, we discussed and admired the architecture of the villas and other properties that had been built in this prime location. These ranged from new, modernistic houses to some magnificent, old and dilapidated villas that were ripe for renovation. As usual, we discussed ideas on how we would tackle such projects if we had the time, money or inclination. It's always nice to dream.

After an hour or so's walk, we reached our destination — an attractive restaurant set just above the beach and decorated in what Kim would describe as "shabby-chic, bohemian style", which kicked off a discussion between her and David on interior design, whilst Yasmin and I talked about interesting things such as what we were going to have for lunch and reminisced about the days when we worked together in Bahrain.

An hour later, when Yasmin and I had had a good chat, Kim and David had totally redesigned our bedroom décor and we'd dispatched a lovely lunch in the sun, we returned home to Yasmin and David's where we spent the rest of what continued to be a beautiful sunny day chilling out and relaxing at the side of the pool. In the evening, Kim and Yasmin went to Alicante airport to collect Yasmin and David's friend Ann who would be taking up residence for a few days. On their return, we all sat down to another one of Yasmin's brilliant dinners.

As may be expected when five friends get together who've not seen each other for some time, the evening continued with us all chatting and boozing well into the early hours. At one point, Ann announced she was planning to celebrate her seventieth birthday at the Glastonbury music festival. Given that Ann is just about the most trendy and glamorous sixty-nine-year-old you could ever wish to meet, the thought of her camping in the mud and rain at Glastonbury came as something of a surprise to me. Good for her, though. I hope I'm still up for doing things like that when I reach her age.

9

Day 6, 12 May

Route: None
Distance today: None
Distance so far: 1,170 kilometres (727 miles)
Bike time: None
Overnight: Yasmin and David's, Denia

I woke up groggily the next morning to find it was another beautiful sunny day with not a cloud in the sky. *Maybe the weather has turned, and we'll get to ride in some decent conditions for the rest of the trip*, I thought hopefully as I donned shorts and T-shirt and headed out to see what was for breakfast.

After one of Yasmin's full English breakfasts, a few coffees and a chat by the side of the pool, I borrowed a bucket and sponge and set off to give Roadie a bit of a clean and check her vitals. I love bikes, but whilst I like mine to look in as pristine a condition as possible, I hate cleaning them. I don't mind cleaning cars because this can be done at either a commercial jet-wash or pretty quickly with a hosepipe, bucket, sponge and a drying cloth at home. A bike, however, and particularly a bike without a fairing to cover up all the mechanical bits, has a million nooks and crannies in which dirt and grime can hide and lots of hard edges that take the skin off your knuckles whilst you're trying to remove it. I learned the results of jet-washing a bike the hard way when I tried it once. The result was a bike that took ages to start after having had high-pressure water blasted all over its vitals and then would only ride at about 40 kph (25 mph) in "limp-home" mode. The dealer later diagnosed a totally fried and very expensive engine control unit. An expensive way of learning that you can't jet-wash a motorcycle.

I acquired my first Harley when I lived in Bahrain. At that time, whilst I'd always maintained my enthusiasm for bikes, I'd not owned one for quite a few years because of the usual reasons of children, mortgages, lack of money, career, etc. During the years of "bike famine", however, I'd borrowed the odd bike for a ride whenever I could, and if I could find somewhere whilst on holiday that rented motorcycles, I would usually take off on my own for a biking day. In Bahrain, however, because my best mate at the time was a lifelong biker and we often used to swap biking stories over a few beers, my enthusiasm had rekindled. At the time, I'd just finished refurbishing a Porsche and was looking for something else to occupy my spare time.

One evening we were at a party, and I was chatting to Johnno, a mate from the rugby club. He was telling me he'd owned a Harley-Davidson for a year but hardly ever got the chance to ride it because he was so busy with his various businesses. I mentioned I had a Porsche that hardly ever got used, and we simultaneously had what was probably an alcohol-induced eureka moment. Would a swap be something that would work for both of us? The next day, and a tad more sober, we met at the rugby club with our respective vehicles. Johnno lent me his helmet, which was about three sizes too big because he was a big bloke who played second row. The helmet, depending on how fast I was going, kept either blowing to the back of my head or falling over my eyes, but I went for a thirty-minute ride.

The feeling of being on a bike is something that's very hard to explain to a non-biker, but bikers just know it — it's a part of them. Excitement, a little danger, a feeling of freedom, the rider involvement that's required to control a bike are all part of this feeling, and during my short ride, all this came back to me in spades. Johnno later told me that, when I arrived back at the club, he knew I was sold on the idea because of the big grin on the part of my face he could see under the droopy helmet. Fortunately, Johnno was also similarly impressed with the Porsche, so we shook on a deal for a straight swap (this was in the days when Porsches weren't worth the silly money they demand these days) and went to the club bar to have a few pints to cement the arrangement. A couple of days later, when paperwork had been exchanged and ownership officially transferred, I was the proud owner of a Harley-Davidson Sportster XL-1200S.

The Sportster came in two engine options — 850cc and 1200cc. Mine was not only the 1200cc version but was a "sport" model. It had twin-plug heads, adjustable gas forks, gas shock absorbers and twin front disc brakes. Forget any images you may have of Italian or Japanese sports bikes with a laid-forward riding position, rear-sets and fairings. The American interpretation of "sport" came with an upright riding position and was a completely naked bike, i.e. no sign of a fairing or any windscreen whatsoever. OK, so I knew it wasn't a proper sports bike when I first saw it, but it definitely looked badass in black paint with a lot of the chrome parts that are fitted to other Sportster models also finished in black. Badass indeed.

Over the next few weeks, I got to know my new toy and burbled about the highways and byways of Bahrain trying to look cool and even a little badass myself as I rediscovered the joys of biking and, even better than that, discovered the joys of biking in a climate that doesn't involve riding in the rain and freezing temperatures, as had been my experience back in the UK.

As I was drying off Roadie, my thoughts wandered back to Bahrain and the days of my Sportster. I couldn't help but remember an ongoing battle I used to have in those days with Razik. He was a lovely Sri Lankan guy who used to look after the house, keep the garden tidy, wash the cars and lived in quarters in the grounds of our villa. When I returned from one of my Friday rides, I always cleaned the bike myself because I enjoyed keeping it looking in pristine condition and found it therapeutic (it was a novelty back in those days). Razik, however, seemed to take this as some sort of challenge, and before too long, he would appear in the garage and start to clean alongside me.

'Razik, you don't need to do this,' I'd say. 'This is Friday, so enjoy your day off.'

'Yes, sir,' he'd reply whilst trying to clean faster than me.

'Razik! Pack it in! I enjoy doing this. No need to help.'

'Yes, sir.' Still polishing and smiling back at me.

I don't know whether Razik just thought it was demeaning for "sir" to do his own bike cleaning, whether I considered him not properly qualified to clean bikes and, therefore, this was a slight on his capabilities, or whether he also loved my bike, but I never did totally win this particular battle. Sometimes, if I left the bike for a while after coming back from a ride, I found he'd beaten me to it, and the Sporty was sitting there gleaming before I'd even had the chance to get the polishing cloths out.

I loved that Sportster, and I took it to Abu Dhabi with me when we moved there. I kept it for four years and eventually sold it, after I'd bought my second Harley, to a guy who was buying on behalf of his friend in India. He planned to have it stripped down and have all the parts sent to India where it would be reassembled to avoid the punitive import duty on vehicles. So, the Sporty began its life in the USA, was sold by the Harley dealers in Saudi Arabia, first registered in Bahrain, exported to the United Arab Emirates and its next country was to be India. The bike had lived in more countries than I had at this point.

Anyway, Roadie was now looking much better, even if not totally up to Razik's standards, so after putting the cleaning stuff away, I wandered into the villa to find we were about to head off into Denia. After a short mooch round town, we found a restaurant in a plaza where we had another long lunch before returning to Yasmin and

David's to finish off the day drinking and chatting until about eleven o'clock.

Slightly worrying was the fact that Kim had spent a long time on the Internet trying to book a place to stay in Barcelona but was finding there was very little availability, and what was available was very expensive.

10

Day 7, 13 May

Route: Denia — Valencia — Castillon — Peñíscola
Distance today: 272 kilometres (169 miles)
Distance so far: 1,442 kilometres (896 miles)
Bike time: 4 hours
Overnight: Porto Cristo Hotel, Peñíscola

You'll recall that the first four days of our trip were spent on the bike in less than clement weather. You'll also recall that the weather for the last two days, which were spent off the bike at Yasmin and David's, had been glorious. I was, therefore, hoping that the rest of the trip would be carried out in the type of weather that southern Spain is famous for, i.e. warm and sunny.

'I don't bloody believe it!' I exclaimed as I opened the curtains on waking up at nine o'clock to see grey, overcast skies over the Montgó. 'It looks miserable out there. Bloody typical now that we're setting off on the bike again!'

'Maybe it will brighten up later? And, seeing you're out of bed, a nice cup of coffee would be good.'

Later, over one of Yasmin's sausage sandwiches and a cuppa, Kim-Dot-Com was still trying to find a place to stay in Barcelona for a reasonable price. 'All I'm finding are three- or four-star hotels for around €250 a night,' she declared. 'It's looking like we'll either have to suck it up and pay through the nose or give Barcelona a miss,' she said as she closed the lid of her laptop.

She had a point. Our research, such as it was, prior to the trip and our past excursions into various parts of Spain had shown us that excellent rooms were available in a variety of good hotels and guesthouses for less than €100 a night, so what was so special about Barcelona? We realised it would be a popular tourist and business destination but didn't expect it to be so popular that hotels could charge two-and-a-half times the normal rate. Very odd!

'We have another day on the road before we get there, so let's make a final decision later,' I replied as I noticed that the window was beginning to get splattered with raindrops. Lovely!

By ten thirty, the bike was packed, and we were ready for the off. With hugs and kisses all round and Yasmin, David and Anne waving goodbye, I fired up the bike and we headed down the Montgó to find the road north towards our next destination of Peñíscola — a name I shouldn't have any difficulty remembering later in the day when I was looking for directions.

We only had around 270 kilometres (167 miles) to cover, so I wanted to keep off the motorways as much as possible and follow the coast road which would take us through a national park and the city of Valencia, after which, depending on how we were feeling, we would have the option of more minor roads or the motorway towards our final destination. Leaving Denia with the sea still on our right (this makes for easy navigation), we headed along the coast road to pass mile after mile of what appeared to be holiday apartments. Although it was the middle of May, only a few showed signs of occupation, and I wondered just how lonely it would be if you lived here all year round and were surrounded by empty dwellings and closed-up cafés, bars and restaurants for most of the time.

The coast road eventually joined up with the main road towards

Valencia. Shortly after we joined the traffic, I noticed a rather strange sight — a middle-aged lady was sitting in a plastic patio chair at the entrance to a lane that led to some farmland. *Maybe she's an orange seller waiting for the oranges to be delivered by the farmer?* I thought and put it out of my mind. A kilometre or so later, however, I spotted another lady sitting on a similar chair, dressed in a short skirt and passing the time by knitting. *Very odd indeed!* The next lady I spotted at the side of the road was a quite a lot younger. She was blonde, dressed in very tight white leggings and was dancing to a ghetto blaster. As we rode along, I spotted several other ladies in similar locations and behaving in the same manner until, finally, the penny dropped.

Prostitution isn't illegal in Spain, and it's fairly common to find "clubs" at the side of main roads or on the outskirts of towns. These aren't, however, gentlemen's clubs of the type that exist in London, nor are they the working men's clubs that are to be found in the North of England, or even dance clubs, but are knocking shops. I suppose they could be regarded as "clubs" in the British sense of the word, but I doubt there would be an old bloke in a flat cap on the door, asking for your union card to prove you were a bonafide working man before you could enter (excuse the pun here — I was going to say "come inside"). It dawned on me that these ladies were, in fact, freelancers waiting for customers, and this realisation immediately caused several questions to pop into my mind.

How much business do they get at eleven thirty in the morning?

Given the fact we're in the middle of the countryside, where do they go to conclude their business?

Do they have a mattress behind the hedge, or is the customer invited to park up further down the lane so that business can be concluded in the car, and if so, what if the customer is a motorcyclist?

Given the fact I don't see any cars parked by the side of the road, how do the ladies get to and from work, and do they bring their patio chairs with them?

How pissed off would you be if you'd concluded a transaction with the middle-aged lady with the knitting and, half an hour later, you spotted the twenty-something blond with the sprayed-on pants?

What was the second lady knitting? Was it something for one of her grandchildren?

How much do they charge?

The phenomenon of roadside hookers at work at midday is possibly unique to the Valencia area because I've never seen it before or since in any other part of Spain. Leaving my rhetorical questions largely unanswered, we burbled steadily along following Satnav Woman's map which led us along diverse highways and byways and eventually to the motorway towards the city of Valencia. We stopped for gas, and the gas station owner showed me photos of his own Harley, and we got chatting about bikes. The guy behind the counter joined in and fired rapid Spanish at me, from which I think the gist was that he wanted to go off on my bike (presumably with my wife), leaving me to work the cash register. This wasn't a great swap from my point of view, but it did make me realise I was quite privileged to even own a Harley and to be able to take three weeks off work to follow a dream. Sadly, for many people, doing such a thing would probably only remain a dream.

The national park to the south of Valencia was uninspiring, even though it contains Spain's largest lake. The area was flat, and a vicious wind was blowing from the coast on our right. This meant two things — firstly, we were still heading in the right direction, and secondly, I was riding with the bike leaning into the wind for most of the way.

Valencia is Spain's third largest city and is also the Mediterranean's largest container port. I'm sure that, like most Spanish towns, it contains many interesting things to see and to do, but we planned to keep moving, and that's what we did. After we'd stopped for coffee and toasties on the outskirts and programmed the GPS, Satnav Woman did an exemplary job of guiding us through the city and onto the road that follows the coast in a north-easterly direction. There are two roads that more or less follow the coast — one being an A-road and the other a motorway toll road. I kept to that day's plan and took the A-road.

So far, although the day had remained overcast, the rain had mercifully held off. This was about to change, however, and about an hour after leaving Valencia, in the vicinity of Castellon de la Plana, I could see we were heading towards an unbroken wall of black, angry-looking clouds. What I usually do in such a situation is employ optimism to keep me dry, i.e. I keep riding in the hope that it won't rain. Of course, by the time I realise my optimism is misplaced, there's no suitable place to stop to put on my wets, and it's already raining. Consequently, I'm usually soaked before I get my waterproofs on, which kind of defeats the object of having them in the first place. Today, however, I decided the sky was so black, it was inevitable we were going to hit some rain, so I pulled over next to a small supermarket where we donned our waterproofs. It didn't take long to get togged up, and before long, we were indeed riding through torrential rain.

We were lucky because, half an hour later, we'd ridden through the storm and, wow, the sun even made an appearance. Whilst we were donning our wets, I'd planned for the worst eventuality and reprogrammed Satnav Woman to take us to Peñíscola by the quickest route, and she'd consequently diverted us onto the toll road. The toll booth was blissfully devoid of traffic, and because of this, I was able to set Roadie's cruise control to a relaxed 120 kph (75 mph), take it easy and admire the lovely, lush countryside with some marvellous vistas opening up before us. Traffic was light to non-existent, and once again, I was reminded that motorway travelling in Spain isn't the tedious drudgery it usually is in other places.

I don't like full-face motorcycle helmets. Yes, I know they're safer and more sensible than other types, but I find they restrict my peripheral vision, become very hot and uncomfortable in high temperatures, and I feel claustrophobic in them. My helmet style of choice is, therefore, an open-face type. I have two helmets, one being a US cop helmet which has a peak, sits above ear level and is the most comfortable helmet I've ever owned. My current helmet is the third of its type I've bought directly from the manufacturer that makes them for the USA police forces. My other helmet is a

Schuberth, open-face, half helmet, which covers my ears and has a flip-up visor. This is good for cooler weather, and the visor makes it good for protection from the elements. I'd thought long and hard about which helmet to use on the trip, and working on the principle that we were only going to have good weather, I was using the cop helmet.

Although the windscreen does a great job of keeping most of the wind and rain off me, it doesn't protect me from absolutely everything. Ouch! Something had hit my forehead in the gap between my helmet and the top of my sunglasses. It stung a little, but I expected it would soon wear off. It didn't. In fact, instead of doing so, it became worse, and my forehead started throbbing. It dawned on me that a bee must have hit me, or more correctly, as I was the one doing 120 kph (75 mph) at the time, *I* had hit a bee. What's more, I must have hit him up the bum and right in the sting. I was tempted to rub the sore spot, but having been stung before, I remembered the sting can become embedded and carries a sac full of poison. If I messed with things with my gloved fingers, I stood a fair chance of just making the situation worse.

I couldn't stop, because we were on a motorway, so I resolved to put up with it until we could either stop and sort it out, or the pain went away. It didn't go away, though. It continued to get even worse until my forehead was throbbing like a blind cobbler's thumb. Splat! What are the odds of two bees hitting you in the finger-width gap between sunglasses and helmet within ten minutes of each other? Pretty long, I would say, so today was *not* my lucky day. Looking on the bright side, the second bee must have head-butted me, because there was no sign of an increase in the throbbing that was the result of being mugged by his mate. Fifteen minutes later, we ran into a search party that was obviously out looking for the missing soldiers because, within a second, the windscreen was covered in half a dozen squashed bees. Are bees like wildebeest? Do they migrate, and is this little corner of Castellon the bee equivalent of the Serengeti? Whatever the reason, they were out in force and weren't looking both ways before crossing the motorway.

Before long, Satnav Woman indicated we should take the next exit and head towards the cost and Peñíscola, so I was able to stop in another handy supermarket car park. Remember when I was ready to start the trip and Kim was still wandering round the house, collecting what seemed to be enough pharmaceuticals to stock Boots the Chemists and that I was possibly a little scathing about this? Well, thank goodness for Nurse Kim because, when I explained what had happened, she went straight to one of the exterior pockets of our bike luggage and withdrew a zip-lock bag containing what appeared to be a full selection of legal drugs and even a magnifying mirror so that I could examine the affected area.

Don't ask me why Nurse Kim didn't examine it for me; she'd probably misplaced her reading glasses or something. With gloves removed, I was able to carefully remove the corpses of two bees and was thankful to see there was no sign of a sting still stuck in my tender flesh. A dab of antihistamine and a ciggie later, and I was ready to hit the road to Peñíscola and our destination for the night. Satnav Woman was perfect and delivered us right to the door of the Porto Cristo Hotel, which we discovered is right beside the attractive-looking beach.

Kim explained that the Porto Cristo was a "boutique hotel". I'm not sure what a boutique hotel is, but it was very likeable, nevertheless, and our room was good, being both furnished and decorated in what presumably could only be described as in a "boutique" style. Having dumped our luggage, and after a quick drink in the hotel bar to wash the travel dust from our throats, we set off to explore. Peñíscola is a resort town with a wide and long beach and everything that goes with that, including hotels, boutiques, boutique hotels, tourist shops, cafés, bars and restaurants. I expect it must become very busy in July and August, but that day it was quiet, and there was a relaxed vibe to it all.

Peñíscola's main claim to fame is that it has its very own castle which is situated on a small peninsula (what did you think they named the town after?) The castle dominates the town, and we could see the citadel, the substantial walls and the houses that cling to the castle's slopes both inside and outside the walls. There have been fortifications on the site of the castle since before Christ, but the Knights Templar built the present castle between 1294 and 1307. The Knights Templar must have had some good builders working for them because, in the days before tower cranes, hard hats and high-viz vests, only thirteen years to build a whole castle, complete with extensive walls, was quite some going.

Rather than hike up the steep slopes of the castle, we elected to have another drink at a beach-front bar and enjoy the view of said castle. I justified this decision to Kim by explaining that, once we'd got to the top, we would only be looking down on the bar that we were sitting in and that, therefore, the vista was better from our current viewpoint.

By now I was getting peckish, so I suggested we should find somewhere for dinner. Peñíscola has an abundance of restaurants, so you would think it would prove to be a simple enough task to find somewhere suitable, but half an hour later, we were still mooching round trying to select somewhere. I use the word "we" somewhat euphemistically here because, if I'm on my own and a place sells food, is not part of a fast-food chain and looks halfway decent, that's where you'll find me tucking into my grub. Not so, however, with my wife, who has a seemingly endless list of boxes that must be ticked before she will deign to grace an eatery with her presence. I usually hold my peace in such situations, but I was tired, my stomach was rumbling with the onset of starvation, and my head was still throbbing.

'So, what was wrong with that one?' I asked, as we walked away from the umpteenth restaurant.

'They only do fish.'

'What about that one?'

'Too expensive.'

'That one?'

'It looks cheap.'
'The one over there?'
'Don't be stupid. It doesn't have a castle view.'
'What about that one?'
'It's an ice cream parlour, idiot!'
'This one?'
'This one? Seriously? Have you seen the colour of the serviettes?'

I don't remember how the final selection was made, or on what particular grounds, but the restaurateurs should have been very proud of themselves to have passed the Kim test. By that time, I could have eaten a scabby dog. I do remember, however, that we had a very satisfying meal accompanied by a good bottle of wine, and as happens so often in Spain, we were pleasantly surprised at the cost when the bill came.

Over dinner, we'd decided that, as Barcelona was on our must-do list for the trip, we would stick to the plan and hang the expense of its seemingly extortionately priced rooms. Once back at the hotel, Kim-Dot-Com declared she would go up to the room to book something, and not wishing to spoil her concentration, I headed to the bar for a nightcap. Given how long it had taken Kim to decide on somewhere to eat, the last thing I expected was to see her entering the bar thirty minutes later, looking as pleased as punch about something and announcing she'd found a good deal on Last-Minute-Good-Hotel-Deals-Dot-Com and had booked us into a modern, 4-star hotel for two nights for a total of €266 instead of the normal price of €440.

At the end of Day 7, we'd travelled further in one week than the distance between Land's End and John O'Groats. That definitely called for a celebratory nightcap or two before heading to bed at around eleven o'clock.

Leaving Yasmin and David's

11

Day 8, 14 May

Route: Peñíscola — Tarragona — Barcelona
Distance today: 243 kilometres (151 miles)
Distance so far: 1,685 kilometres (1,046 miles)
Bike time: 4 hours 15 minutes
Overnight: Tryp Hotel Condal Mar, Barcelona

There's basically only one route to take for most of the journey between Peñíscola and Barcelona, and that's the AP-7 motorway for about two thirds of the way and then a choice between staying on the motorway or taking the C-32 which hugs the coastline. I didn't have a plan except to see how I was feeling when it was time to choose between the two.

We'd woken up at eight o'clock, and guess what? Blue skies greeted me as I opened the curtains to see what the weather was doing. Yay! Kim was in bed with her morning coffee, researching hotels on the Internet for our destination after Barcelona, which would need to be just south of the French border and close to the

Furthest Point East at Cap de Creus. I decided to have a shower whilst she continued with her research.

Two minutes later, I let out a loud yell as I was deluged with freezing cold water.

'What's wrong with you?' asked my beloved from the bedroom.

'The bloody shower just dumped cold water on me,' I replied and continued to chunter my dissatisfaction to myself.

'Stop moaning and get on with it, you wuss.'

I find that hotel bathrooms are often a source of irritation. Housekeeping never seems to tell maintenance about the wobbly toilet seat, the blocked sink or dripping tap, but my major gripe is shower controls. Once upon a time, we had the mixer valve, which was good because it was simple. You had one knob to control the flow of water and one knob to control the temperature, and each knob was clearly labelled so that everyone knew which knob did what. Not so these days and another example of how "progress" often makes things worse. Shower valve manufacturers seem to be in a competition to make the most complicated controls possible, but for what reason? Surely, they can't be deliberately setting out to boil people alive or to ensure they only have cold showers. Worse than that is the sneaky lever that, when you push, turn or pull it, results in the shower immediately, and without prior warning, douching you with cold water as was the cause of my gripe here. As a construction industry person, not only does my mind boggle at the total incompetence of such designers but also the idiocy of the lunatics that specify such things for their hotels. Kim admitted that, in one of the hotels we stayed in, she never did discover how to operate the shower and ended up having to take a bath instead. If I had my way, hotel designers would be made to spend time as customers in the hotels rooms they've designed so they realise just how useless they are at their jobs.

I cheered up and stopped chuntering, however, when I discovered that the shampoo, shower gel and the other bottle you always get but never use, all had writing on them that was large enough to read. Based on this, I decided not to be a picky old git about the shower and suggested to Kim that she give the hotel an excellent review on Booking.com.

After a breakfast at the hotel (it was probably included in the price this time), we were on the road by nine forty-five and heading towards the AP-7. Despite spending a lot of time in Spain and having travelled there quite extensively, I've never got the hang of the Spanish road-numbering system. In the UK, we have a good system — "M" stands for motorway, "A" stands for A-class roads that are either dual carriageways or major roads, "B" stands for windy, country-type lanes where your speed will be fairly limited, and everything else is unclassified, so not really worth bothering about. Quite a simple, but adequate, system. In Spain, however, we have A, AP, B, GI, GIV, GIP, N, SE and probably others that my quick look on Google Maps didn't reveal. In an Internet post, one person simply said he 'would describe the Spanish numbering system as a total shambles.' One thing I do know is that, if it has a "P" in the name, "P" stands for "pay" or, if you want to get continental about it, "*peage*", which is quite logical because the Spanish word for "to pay" is *pagar*.

I don't object to paying to travel on well-maintained roads which, presumably because the Spanish would rather not pay for the privilege, are quite lightly trafficked. I reckon that, if you consider the fuel consumption and wear and tear on your car or bike whilst maintaining a steady 120 kph (75 mph) in top gear on a motorway and compare this with the amount of acceleration, braking and gear changing that's necessary on an A-road, the tolls aren't as costly as you may think. I don't suppose, however, that many people think like that. In fact, I know several who won't use the toll road for a forty-minute journey between the area where we live and Faro and would rather take twice as long to get there on a badly-maintained, single-lane road which passes through several small towns en route. If you add the stress factor of a longer and more difficult drive, the toll road makes even more sense. Anyway, I usually pay the tolls automatically by credit card, and as we all know, that's not the same as spending proper money.

It's amazing what a bit of sunshine does for your mood at any time, but when you're on a bike, this is multiplied by a factor of many. I was, consequently, more than happy to set off under clear, blue, sunny skies for the first time on our trip. It was a little windy, but hey, the sunshine more than compensated for that.

Unfortunately, this happy state of affairs wasn't to last for very long, and as we rode further north, the wind increased to a very big number on the Beaufort scale and, in addition to its sheer force, was also coming in unpredictable gusts. It was pushing the bike all over the road, roaring in my ears and trying to force my helmet off my head and my head off my shoulders — not much fun then! To add insult to injury, and as if I didn't already know it was blowing a gale, the helpful Spanish authorities had erected signs and airfield-type windsocks every few kilometres. Obviously, windy conditions weren't unusual along this stretch of road. The signs helpfully warned motorists that it could get windy hereabouts, and the windsocks indicated the strength of the wind. I didn't need a sign to tell me it was windy, or a windsock to tell me the wind was strong, because both factors were totally obvious. This was the equivalent of spending public money on signs to tell you it gets dark at night.

The wind made it impossible for me to relax and enjoy what would otherwise have been a great ride. The sun was still shining. We could see the shimmering sea to our right (*good — we're still heading anti-clockwise then*) and some pretty impressive mountains to our left. *Think positive — at least it's not raining!*

After only an hour or so, I needed a break, and Roadie needed gas, so I had an excuse to pull into a service station. We sat outside with our coffees, and even there, the wind was still giving us a battering. After a while and back on the bike, the hurricane we'd been experiencing thankfully died down to just a moderate gale. We eventually left the toll road just past Tarragona and followed the coast road towards Barcelona. What a great decision that proved to be. This is a fantastic road which hugs the coast and goes in and out of tunnels carved through the hilly terrain. To our left, we had a verdant green forested landscape, and to our right, constant views of the Mediterranean. This road more than made up for me having wind (so to speak) earlier in the day.

As we approached Barcelona, I remembered our hotel was on the northern side of the city, and we were approaching from the south, so by my reckoning, we would have to ride through the centre of Spain's second largest city to reach our hotel. Hmm!

One of the downsides about touring is that, inevitably, you'll arrive in a large, strange city and have to find your destination during rush hour. Due to the dense traffic, much of your time is spent travelling at walking pace, which is never a fun thing to do on a bike because, whilst motorcycles are quite stable at speed, they're a bit tricky to balance at very slow speeds, especially when riding two-up and heavily laden with luggage. Kim and I have developed a system we use to deal with navigating our way through strange cities in rush hour. I concentrate on controlling the bike, keeping it upright, making sure I'm in the right lane for where we want to go, watching for pedestrians, avoiding other vehicles and crazy scooter and moped riders who know where they're going, checking for traffic signals, pedestrian crossings, street signs, direction signs and trying to follow the route suggested by Satnav Woman. Kim's role is to tap me on the shoulder occasionally and tell me she thinks I'm heading in the wrong direction.

On this occasion, because I didn't have my Schuberth helmet that connects me both to the intercom system in Kim's helmet and to Satnav Woman's incredibly posh voice via Bluetooth, I would be totally reliant on Satnav Woman's map, so I would have to keep an eye on that as well as maintaining 360-degree awareness and 100-per cent concentration on the road conditions. The upside to this would be that neither Kim nor Satnav Woman could shout at me through the intercom system to tell me I'd taken a wrong turn.

I needn't have worried. Even though Satnav Woman guided us along a route that took us straight through the centre of the city, I was pleasantly surprised to find the roads were well planned and laid out, and the traffic, although heavy, kept moving at a good pace. This was achieved by having a six-lane road through the city centre. It wasn't a motorway but a proper urban road with traffic signals, pedestrian crossings and suchlike, and whereas in most cities, you lurch from one red light to the next, the system here was that you passed through three or four signals on green before having to stop at red for a while. Fantastic!

Leaving the city centre, I missed the turning to take us to our hotel, but after turning at the next junction, Satnav Woman guided us flawlessly back to the Tryp Hotel Condal Mar, where we arrived at around two o'clock. As usual, I unpacked the bike and noted down Roadie's mileage for my log whilst Kim checked us in. I later worked out that, on our trip so far, we'd covered the same distance as London to Madrid.

The Hotel Condal Mar was a well-appointed, modern hotel, and we decided to have a late lunch in the restaurant before setting out to explore Barcelona. The menu in the restaurant was extensive with some good Spanish cuisine, so I had to smile a little when I noticed a British family all tucking into burgers and chips accompanied by pints of lager.

Looking at the map we obtained from reception, we realised we weren't too far from the coast, so we headed in that direction with the intention of getting a bit of exercise. When we got there, we found that Barcelona has its very own beach. Imagine that! I couldn't think of another city with a population of 1.7 million that has its own beach. (OK, now I've thought a bit more, Sydney and Rio probably qualify.)

As we walked along the promenade, we saw exercise stations, cafés, skateboard and BMX bike parks; all sorts of things for the people of Barcelona to enjoy. I thought it was a splendid thing for the municipality to have provided these facilities and rather sadly reflected on the fact that, if this was the UK, everything would probably have been vandalised.

Remember how I said this was the first day we'd ridden in sunshine? Well, just to show us that the weather gods hadn't forgotten how to put a damper on things, it began to rain, and to rain quite heavily at that. The good thing about being in a city when it rains is there's always somewhere on hand in which to shelter. In our case, this turned out to be a bar, where we ordered a couple of drinks and whiled away the time watching people getting soaked and the rain bouncing off the pavement outside.

Eventually the rain stopped, and we continued to follow the beach on our walk. The beach goes on for a long way and, eventually, ends at Barcelona's port area, which is just about where we reached when it started to lash it down again. This time, shelter was found in a scruffy restaurant serving pretty basic fast food, where Kim was definitely not happy and seemed to refuse to accept the simple fact that, by the time we'd found a better place, we would be soaked through as my justification for diving through the door. I ate my pizza accompanied by that stony silence that lets you know you're currently not the flavour of the month. Kim steadfastly refused to eat anything and collected one more point towards her gold Joan of Arc badge.

Pizza consumed, it was still raining cats and dogs, or as the Spanish say, *"Está lloviendo a cántaros"* (it's raining jugfuls). We grabbed a taxi back to the hotel and, to celebrate the fact we were speaking again, popped into the bar to celebrate our renewed marital bliss. Surveying the lively bar, I immediately noticed that half the clientele was wearing Ferrari, Mercedes, McLaren and other motor-racing shirts. Hearing a guy order a round of drinks in English, I asked him what was going on. It turned out this was the weekend of the Spanish Grand Prix, and the circuit was just outside Barcelona. Later, whilst chatting to a Spanish couple, we also learned that

Monday and Tuesday were to be a public holiday in Spain. We now realised why hotel rooms were so hard to find and were so expensive. Well done, Kim-Dot-Com, for even finding us a room, much less finding one in an excellent hotel at a very reasonable price. She does like a bargain!

Templar castle, Peñíscola

Day 9, 15 May

Route: None
Distance today: None
Distance so far: 1,685 kilometres (1,046 miles)
Bike time: None
Overnight: Tryp Hotel Condal Mar, Barcelona

I'm not a fan of big cities, and here we were in Barcelona, Spain's second largest city, which has over three times the population of our home town of Sheffield. Although I grew up in the UK's fourth largest city, I was always lucky enough to live on the outskirts and to be close to the countryside, so I spent my younger years surrounded by woods, fields and other green stuff. Even after Kim and I were married, we always lived within striking distance of the Peak District National Park and spent many happy days hiking in this beautiful area. After the kids were born, our weekends often involved trips to the country or walking through Sheffield's many parks. Although Kim does like searching for bargains and mooching round the shops, I'm not much of a shopper, so the average city centre has little appeal to me. What I really dislike about cities is the fact that you can't walk more than about five paces without some idiot suddenly stopping dead in their tracks or veering across your path to look at a pair of shoes in a shop window. As one of James Herriot's characters, who'd spent a lifetime as a farmer walking the Yorkshire moors, said of towns, 'I went to Leeds once but didn't reckon nowt to it. I had to take big steps and littluns all t'time.'

Even interesting cities that have lots of historical stuff going on tend to get on my nerves after a short while because the very fact that they have lots of historical stuff going on means they also have lots of tourists looking at the historical stuff, clogging up the areas where the historical stuff is and generally getting in my way whilst they take selfies. I would generally forgo the cultural aspects of even our great cities (with the possible exception of Madrid, Istanbul and Rome), because I find that the tourists make them a pain in the backside. I will, however, make an exception for Barcelona, which (again, with the possible exception of Madrid, Istanbul and Rome) is one of the few cities to which I would be happy to return.

The day didn't get off to a great start. Kim was researching "ten best things to do in Barcelona" on the Internet before we went down for breakfast and asked me to check a few things on a website she'd discovered and to book tickets online for a couple of attractions whilst she got ready. I was gasping for my first nicotine fix of the day and was keen to get downstairs and outside the hotel to spark up a cigarette.

'It'll be OK,' I said as I grabbed my Marlboros and headed towards the door. 'We'll get tickets when we get there. See you at breakfast.'

Over breakfast, Kim advised me that all the advice she'd read on the Internet was to pre-book tickets for the major tourist attractions, and that, if we couldn't buy them on site when turning up on spec, 'IT WILL BE ALL YOUR FAULT.' Well, what's new there then?

Our first stop after a long but invigorating walk from the hotel was the cathedral Sagrada Família which is something of a must-see in Barcelona. Its full name is Basílica i Temple Expiatori de la

Sagrada Família, and construction was started in 1882, and get this — it's still not finished! I know builders are always late, and I've spent the latter part of my career analysing why this is so and finding excusable reasons for their delays. I have, however, never in my investigations come across a case where the private donations necessary for the funding kept running out or that the work was suspended because of the Spanish Civil War. The cathedral was designed by Catalan architect Antoni Gaudí who worked on it until he died after being hit by a tram in 1926. The design has stayed pretty faithful to what I assume, from seeing other examples of his work, was Gaudí's original concept. That's to say, pretty damn weird. Gaudí once said that his client, God, was in no hurry to see it finished, and I've never heard that excuse used before either.

They say a picture is worth a thousand words, so do me a favour and Google the Sagrada Família now because this will save me from a lot of typing that will never even come close to adequately describing what essentially looks like something that Tolkien, Disney or George Lucas may have dreamed up. On second thoughts, maybe Tolkien, Disney or George Lucas got their inspiration from Gaudí, which just goes to show exactly how weird this incredible building is. One of the classic music albums of all time is the Beatles' *Sergeant Pepper's Lonely Hearts Club Band*, and it's widely accepted that, apart from the absolute genius of the Beatles themselves, one of the reasons this album broke totally new musical ground was that the Beatles were experimenting with hallucinogenic drugs at the time. Well, if Lennon and McCartney were on acid when they wrote "Lucy In the Sky with Diamonds", God knows what Gaudí was on when he came up with the Sagrada Família, and it's a holy place, too! Did you Google it? Do you see what I mean?

I've also just Googled it and found that the *Tourist Guide to Barcelona* advises that, not only is the Sagrada Família famous for being Barcelona's No.1 tourist attraction, it's also famous for its long entrance queues. The guide also offers advice on how best to avoid the queues, but I didn't bother checking this because I'm pretty sure they would have told me to pre-book on the Internet, which is exactly what Kim may have also possibly mentioned as soon as we rolled up and saw the extent of the ticket queues, which were huge. *Oops!* I thought, *I'm in for it now. Maybe my first smoke of the day is going to be harmful to my health in more ways than the government warnings envisage.*

The mass of tourists here meant this had a similar look to the Vatican about it. We'd visited the Vatican earlier in the year when we went to Rome to see Italy and England play in the Six Nations Rugby Championship. (We won again, yay!) The whole experience (the Vatican, that is, not the rugby) was spoiled for us by the sheer numbers of people the authorities had managed to cram into the place. By way of comparison, moving through the palace felt very much like leaving a rugby stadium after a match; you had no choice but to keep moving forward, shoulder to shoulder with your fellow visitors.

I'm not a religious person, but to my way of thinking, the Vatican should be a place where believers may take their time to experience the essence of the most important symbol of Christianity, and people who aren't religious may take their time to appreciate and contemplate the wonderful artworks. The long and short of our experience was that we hardly saw anything (sorry, Michelangelo, I wanted to see how the ceiling turned out), because we couldn't wait to get out of the place.

Back in Barcelona, the upshot of our experience at the Vatican was that, having seen how busy it was, even Kim wasn't bothered about going inside — phew! So we contented ourselves with marvelling at Gaudí's work from the exterior whilst drinking the most expensive cup of coffee in the world and contemplating whether tourists deliberately set out to wear such stupid clothes, or if they just do it by accident. We had saved the cost of the tickets that we would have bought, had I followed instructions and pre-booked online, which went some way towards compensating us for the price of the coffee.

Whilst sipping our coffees, we noticed there were plenty of open-topped tourist buses dropping off and collecting passengers, so to make amends for what Kim seemed to consider to be my earlier disinterest in touristic matters, I wandered over to a ticket office and found out that a ticket would last all day. We could get on and off at will and swap between routes, and there would even be a free audio commentary as the bus wound its way round the various sights. I don't remember the cost, but I most likely thought that, if this got me out of Kim's bad books, it would be worth it, so off we went.

The Park de Güell was close to the bus route and seemed like it might be a tranquil place to chill out for a while, and its situation on a hill overlooking the city and beyond that to the Mediterranean promised some good photo opportunities. We knew it was on a hill because it was a stiff fifteen-minute uphill walk from where the bus dropped us. Any thoughts of tranquillity were soon dispelled as we saw yet more hordes of tourists. The park contains the Gaudí museum (yes, him again) and, guess what? We couldn't get tickets for the museum on site, so we had to be content with a wander round the park and a look inside Gaudí's old house. We learned that the park (which is rather impressive) was originally part of a commercially unsuccessful housing site which was the idea of Count Eusebi Güell who obviously took the opportunity to big himself up by naming it after himself.

Güell intended to take advantage of the clean, fresh air in this location, which was well away from smoky factories, and make the most of the beautiful views from the site and provide sixty plots for luxury houses. Ultimately, only two houses were built. (What is it with these Spanish builders?) One was intended to be a show house which, on being completed in 1904, was put up for sale. As no buyers came forward, Gaudí, at Güell's suggestion, bought it (I bet he got a really good deal) and he lived there with his family from 1906 to 1926. The house is now the Casa Museu Gaudí (Gaudí House Museum). The park itself was designed by, guess who? Yep, that Gaudí bloke again.

Hopping back on the bus for a short trip, we alighted in the city centre, and now we'll come to why I love Barcelona so much. The city centre is delightful and has a very special feeling which isn't only due to its lovely buildings but the sense of space it provides. If you end up on La Rambla, which is one of the main thoroughfares, you'll find yourself on a 1.2-kilometre (0.7-mile) pedestrianised boulevard which is bordered by many magnificent buildings dating back to the 1800s which contain a variety of interesting shops (well, as interesting as shops ever get). Pavement cafés are shaded under twin rows of trees, and the area attracts street performers to entertain visitors. Many of the buildings in this area were designed by, guess who? Yep, our old mate Gaudí, and this lends another area of interest and quirkiness to the city centre. By this time, I was beginning to like Barcelona and like it a lot.

Whilst Gaudí undoubtedly made an important contribution to Barcelona, the real credit must go to Ildefons Cerdà. In the mid-nineteenth century, Barcelona was similar to many large cities of the time. That's to say, overcrowded, unsanitary, epidemic-ridden, dirty and, well, a bit of a mess. Cerdà drew up plans to expand the city limits outside the old city walls and must have possessed an uncannily futuristic vision, because his design still works one hundred and fifty years later. The principles he incorporated into the design were to provide sunlight and natural ventilation in homes, the need for greenery in the inhabitant's surroundings, efficient waste disposal and the need for movement of people, goods, energy and information. The result is a city centre that's superbly laid out on a grid system where the generously wide streets have plenty of room for both vehicles and pedestrians, which is something seldom seen in any large city.

We lived in Dubai for a number of years where significant development and expansion of the city started only about twenty-five years ago. Because all the expansion was on virgin land, the planners and designers were able to start with a blank sheet of paper, so you would think things would be fairly easy. Constant changes and additions to the infrastructure and many traffic problems proved, however, that even with this starting point, they still didn't get it anywhere near as right as Cerdà did with Barcelona one hundred and fifty years earlier.

After grabbing a spot of lunch and people-watching for a while in these splendid surroundings, we hopped back on the tour bus which would take us to the Plaza de España which Yasmin and David had told us was well worth a visit. As the bus wound its way along the route, we noticed an extraordinary number of Barcelona football fans congregating in the streets. The police and municipality were erecting barriers and closing certain roads off to traffic. Barcelona and Catalan flags abounded, and there was a real party atmosphere in the air.

The bus reached the outskirts of the city and wound its way up a hill into a large park-like area which we thought was worth a stop-off and a stroll, so we alighted at what we later found out was the National Art Museum of Catalonia. I can't vouch for its artworks because we didn't go inside, but the building and its setting are magnificent. The museum is set on the top of a hill and looks down over a series of fountains and waterfalls to the Plaza de España far below. When we looked down, all we saw was a sea of blue and red Barcelona shirts flooding the square. After making our way towards the square and snapping away with the camera, we had no choice but to join the throngs of Barca fans. I asked a lady what was happening, and she explained that the day before had been the last matches of the season, and the results of the games decided whether Barca or Real Madrid would be league champions. Well, no prizes for guessing who won, so there was to be a victory parade by the Barca players and the Plaza de España would be where it ended. The fans were waiting to get a glimpse of their heroes and to celebrate along with them.

I'm not really a football fan. As far as I'm concerned, it's a game played by over-paid prima donnas who seem more concerned about their hairstyles than anything else. I also dislike the fact that, at least in some countries, football tends to attract the hooligan element of society. What I saw here was a far cry from my personal image of football and reminded me more of a rugby crowd. All generations were present, from the very old to the very young, and this was a real family affair. People sat around, enjoying picnics, drinking beer and the only "atmosphere" here was one of happiness and celebration.

We hung around for an hour or so enjoying the party feeling and then, being caught up in the occasion, decided to walk along the parade route back towards the city centre. Eventually, the victory bus came in sight but quite a long way in the distance down a long boulevard. If we hadn't been able to see the bus, we would have still known it was close because of the singing and cheering that accompanied it. We decided to take an outside table at a bar so that we could watch it pass, but what we hadn't anticipated was that hundreds of fans walking alongside were following their heroes, so we were soon swamped by a sea of bodies, all chanting and singing their team songs. I dare say that, in other circumstances, I would have felt a little uneasy at being totally surrounded by football fans, but on this occasion, I just joined in the smiles and the cheering. I managed to get a few photos of the players on the open-topped bus and sent them to our son, Nik, and son-in-law, Matt, for bragging rights and to see if they recognised anyone. 'All of them,' came the reply from Nik a few minutes later. I also sent the photos to an ex-colleague who, despite being from Jordan, is a huge Real Madrid fan. His reply was somewhat less than complimentary towards the Barca players.

As we sat finishing our beers, we were most impressed by the fact that, following close on the heels of the victory bus and the fans, was a municipality cleaning team who were cleaning up the debris left behind by the throngs. Ten minutes after the parade had passed, everything was spick and span, and you would never have noticed a major party had just taken place. Brilliant!

We continued to walk towards the city centre and, just by following our noses, ended up in the Gothic Quarter which is the old town of Barcelona. In total contrast to the city centre, this area is made up of winding, narrow, cobbled streets with tall, old buildings.

Apparently, Picasso lived and worked here for around ten years. Had he been around a little earlier, he would probably have been good mates with Gaudí because, to my untrained eye at least, their work contains many similarities. Following our noses still further, we arrived at Port Olympic which was substantially redeveloped in 1992 for, as the name suggests, the Barcelona Olympics. Part of this district contains an area brimming with restaurants, bars and cafés which was exactly what we needed after a very long day.

Considering that all day long we'd tramped the streets of Barcelona under the hot sun (it was another non-riding day, so what did you expect?) and we were, by this time, just about dead on our feet, you could be forgiven for thinking we would just find a likely-looking restaurant so that we could take the weight off our feet, order a drink and a meal and generally celebrate what had been a thoroughly enjoyable day. Kim was, however, on another mission to find the perfect restaurant, so we had to make a couple of circuits of the area to examine the establishments, study their menus and check the colour of their serviettes before we eventually settled on an Italian restaurant. Italian? Well, what else in one of Spain's most agreeable cities?

Toasting ourselves after dinner, we both agreed this had been a brilliant day and that Barcelona is a fantastic city, and we vowed to go back and spend more time there. It was, therefore, two very weary but happy travellers who arrived back at their hotel at eleven thirty and collapsed into bed, totally exhausted.

National Art Museum of Catalonia

13

Day 10, 16 May

Route: Barcelona — Girona — Figueres — Cadaqués
Distance today: 177 kilometres (110 miles)
Distance so far: 1,862 kilometres (1,157 miles)
Bike time: 3 hours
Overnight: Hostal Marina, Cadaqués

After our exhausting but thoroughly enjoyable day in Barcelona, we slept like the dead until nine thirty the next morning. Our destination that day was to be somewhere near to Cap de Creus, the Furthest Point East, but Kim wasn't finding much on the Internet in the way of accommodation in this area, and everything half decent seemed to be booked up again, probably due to the public holiday. It was only around 175 kilometres (108 miles) to Cap de Creus, so we decided to head in that direction and look for something as and when we felt ready to stop for the day. There were some fairly large towns in the general vicinity, so we figured we would probably have a good chance of finding somewhere on the road after we'd ticked off the Furthest Point East. After breakfast at the hotel, we were packed up, checked out and ready to hit the road by eleven thirty —almost midday! We seemed to be getting later as the trip progressed.

For once, the weather gods were being kind to us, and it was a beautiful day. That's to say, calm, sunny and warm, but not too hot and with hardly a cloud in the sky. This was Day 10 of our trip, so it was about time we had some decent weather on a riding day. Our route took us out of Barcelona without a hitch and along the AP-7, another sparsely trafficked toll road. I set the cruise control to a comfortable speed and relaxed into a lovely ride and made the most of the sunny weather.

We saw quite a lot of Harleys on the road that day. Possibly, this was due to it being a public holiday, but I'd also noticed a few groups of riders on non-Spanish-registered bikes, so I wondered what was going on. We'd already passed a large group of Polish-registered bikes on our way out of Barcelona, and when we stopped for gas and coffee at a service station, there were several Harleys parked up, including a group of guys with Swedish plates on their bikes. Wandering across and saying hello, I asked them if they were having a good trip, and we swapped a few bike stories. I found out they'd attended a Harley rally in the vicinity over the weekend. I had to take my hat off to them because Stockholm to Barcelona is a trip of 2,800 kilometres (1,740 miles). We'd been on the road for ten days and had only so far done around 1,800 kilometres (1,118 miles). The Swedish bikes were heavily customised which is something that's fairly normal for Scandinavian bikes. This is because of the long winters and the short riding season which mean that bikes are usually off the road during the long, dark winters, and their owners get their biking fix by working on them. One of the guys was riding a hard-tail chopper. Hard-tail means the bike has a rigid frame and no rear suspension and is usually only seen on bikes that are primarily for show rather than go. This guy was obviously from pure Viking stock because a 5,600-kilometre (3,480-mile) round trip wouldn't be something that many people would attempt on a touring bike, much less a hard-tail. Big respect.

Back on the road, the motorway bypassed Girona and headed

northwards towards Figueres where we could see some impressive mountains to our left. I wondered if these were the Pyrenees, where we would be heading after Cap de Creus, or another range. Spain has a lot of mountains. Whatever they were, they provided a magnificent backdrop to this part of the ride.

After Girona, we passed a commercial park at the side of the motorway where we spotted that one of the outlets had a big advertising sign on its wall advising passers-by it was a sex supermarket. Unfortunately, there wasn't an exit close to this rather unusual shop, so we couldn't nip in to check it out. As we rode on, however, my imagination began to envisage what a sex supermarket would be like. I pictured customers pushing their shopping trolleys up and down aisles and browsing the shelves stocked with a wide variety of sex toys of all shapes and sizes. 'Excuse me. Could you direct me to the strap-on section please?' or 'Excuse me. Do you have this in a larger size?' Couples would be shopping together; him pushing the trolley round whilst she moved from shelf to shelf examining the goods, reading the labels, comparing prices and popping the occasional selection into the trolley. 'Honey, I got a real bargain there. These nipple clamps cost €10 more in our sex supermarket back home.' As with any supermarket, lady customers would stop without warning and abandon their trolley in the middle of an aisle, making it impossible for anyone to pass when they spotted a particular type of butt plug they'd been trying to find for a while.

There would be a clothing section with racks of naughty-nurse outfits and basques which make the best of wonderful cleavages. Maybe a lady would be checking the mirror outside the fitting rooms to see if her bum looked big in a black latex catsuit. Possibly, there would even be special offers along the lines of "This week's special! Rampant Rabbits — 2 for 1." On completing your weekly shop and taking your trolley to the checkout, I wondered if the bored-looking cashier would ask if you wanted cashback or make a comment on your purchases along the lines of, 'Mmm! Thai beads. Good choice,' as she scanned the barcode.

A few kilometres before Figueres, Satnav Woman directed me to take the next exit and then to follow the road east towards Cap de Creus, some 40 kilometres (24 miles) away. I don't know if there was a less direct but less severe road to our destination, but as we progressed, the road became narrower and windier, and we found ourselves riding alongside sheer drops which were giving me vertigo. This made the road to Ronda look like an A-road, and with what had happened to us on that particular road very much in the forefront of my mind, I rode very gingerly and felt a real wuss when two guys on sports bikes blasted past us and hit a series of bends at what looked like twice our speed.

I felt very nervous on this road, which is something I'd hardly ever felt on a motorcycle for many years. Was it the constant bends, the huge drops just a few metres away, the narrowness of the road or the fact that we were two-up on a bike packed with luggage? I've happily scraped my footboards whilst riding through mountains in the Middle East, Yosemite National Park and the Alps, and on these occasions, Kim had often been with me and we'd been carrying luggage. What was causing me to ride like a beginner then? There was just no fluidity to my riding. I was braking at the wrong time, and the bike was up and down whilst negotiating bends instead of going round smoothly at more or less the same angle of lean. The further I rode, the worse I seemed to get, and I was thankful to reach the town of Cadaqués where, spotting a few cafés, restaurants and a motorcycle parking area, I pulled up and parked the bike.

'What was wrong there?' Kim asked. 'That wasn't like you. Normally, you would've loved a road like that, but you seemed very uncomfortable today.'

'You're right. I wasn't happy, but I have no idea why,' was my bemused reply.

'Well, we got here safely, and that's the main thing,' said Kim, putting a positive spin on things. 'Let's go and get some lunch.'

Cadaqués is in the centre of a large bay, so we selected a beachside restaurant and began to examine our surroundings, which were quite lovely. The small town is set in a natural bay and reminded me in some respects of fishing villages in Devon and Cornwall, with tall headlands with sheer cliffs at either side of the bay and houses built right to the water's edge. We could see both fishing and pleasure boats moored in various areas round the bay. The place had an upmarket, touristy feel to it, and we decided it definitely had our stamp of approval.

'How about trying to find somewhere to stay here for the night?' suggested Kim. 'I'm still tired out after yesterday in Barcelona, so why don't we chillax here for a couple of days?'

Why not indeed? I thought. 'That sounds like a good plan.'

'OK. You stay here and relax for a bit, and I'll have a wander round and see if I can find us somewhere to stay.'

Not knowing whether we'd finished riding for the day, which would mean I could have a beer, or whether we would need to ride further, I ordered another coffee, and as I sipped it, admired the various bikes pulling in and out of the motorcycle parking area just across the road. Remembering it was a public holiday, it seemed the bikers had probably come here just to have fun on the road that had only recently caused me to lose my mojo, because that's what bikers like to do on their days off. Well, that's what proper bikers do, anyway. I was beginning to question whether I was still a proper biker if I could no longer handle a road such as the one we'd just ridden.

The fact that that day and the next were a public holiday got me thinking about the Spanish attitude to holidays and work in general. It isn't quite the same as in the UK and, I dare say, the rest of Northern Europe. I was once trying to organise a time to take my car into the garage across the border in Spain to have a small job attended to and found out that the rest of the week was a public holiday. On seeing my disappointed look, my Spanish friend Meri asked me how many public holidays we have in the UK. My guess was about ten days, but further research revealed that, in a normal year with no royal jubilees or the like, the UK has eight days. With the exception of Christmas Day, Boxing Day and New Year's Day, all bank holidays are scheduled to take place on a Monday, or in the case of Good Friday, as you may expect, on a Friday. This allows the UK population to have long weekends which is a pretty good way of organising things. Maybe I should have said it's a good way of organising things if you want to keep the population at work and contributing to the economy.

Not so in Spain. If a holiday is scheduled on, say, the thirteenth of the month then, whatever day of the week this falls on, the thirteenth is the day that it takes place. You may think that the authorities would arrange things so the Spanish have long weekends too, but no, the Spanish take what are known as "bridge days" in addition to the actual public holidays. I'm not sure whether this is official or just customary, but it basically means that, if a holiday falls on, let's say, a Thursday, the thinking is, 'What's the point of going to back to work on Friday, so let's take Friday off too.' As well as national holidays, the various regions in Spain have their own celebrations, and often towns or smaller areas have even more. The upshot of all this is, as Meri explained to me, that the inhabitants of our local town have around thirty days' holiday per year in addition to their vacations. Great for the employees and school children, but not so good for businesses and industry who presumably have to pay salaries during these holidays.

Something else that strikes me as being fairly unusual are the hours that some people work. I guess you all know about the Spanish afternoon siesta. Consequently, shops and businesses are very often closed between around 1 and 4 p.m. To be fair, the businesses are often open until around 8 p.m., so most people do work a nine-hour day. I say "most people" here, because I think that one of the best jobs to have in Spain is either in a public office where the hours are from eight in the morning to three in the afternoon, or even better, a bank whose hours are eight thirty to two.

You may think all this is a bit of a moan about the Spanish way of life, but it isn't. The point I'm trying to make here is that Northern Europeans and, I dare say, other nationalities elevate work to a much higher level of importance than the Spanish and many other Mediterranean countries. In my opinion, having adequate time to socialise with friends and family is much more important than working hard to be able to afford all the things that advertising and marketing tell us are essential to leading a fulfilling life.

The social aspect of the Spanish way of life is further enabled because eating out is very cheap compared to Northern Europe, so people spend a substantial amount of time in cafés, bars and restaurants, again spending time with friends and family. The majority of the Spanish also tend not to be as materialistic as those in Northern Europe. Smaller houses work because people spend so much time outdoors, and older, small, economical cars tend to be much more common than in other countries. Living in Spain and Portugal has made me realise that quality of life is not so much what you have in material things, but how you enjoy it, and that the things that often provide this type life are either free — like good weather, taking a walk on the beach — or inexpensive — such as having a couple of beers whilst watching the world go by in a pavement café. Spain helped me to find what, to me at least, was an alternative way of doing things, and I think it's a better way. Having said that, I'm glad I live in a lovely villa, have three decent cars and two Harleys.

After I'd spent some time contemplating the quality of life and how much I'd come to enjoy living in Spain and Portugal, Kim wandered back. 'I've just checked the hotel over there,' she said, pointing to the Hostal Marina, overlooking the beach. 'They only have one room left. It's a bit basic, but I checked the room. It's clean and has a lovely balcony, and it's only €80 a night.'

'Sounds good to me. Let's do it then,' I replied, before asking the waiter for the bill.

'The guy on reception said we could park the bike right outside, so we won't have to hump the luggage very far, and you can keep an eye on the bike from the room.'

The Hostal Marina was, indeed, quite basic but clean, with a generously sized room and, as promised by Kim, a lovely, large balcony with a view over the town and the bay. So far on the trip, we'd stayed in fairly upmarket places costing over €100 per night, so the somewhat basic accommodation here was a bit of a change, but as we'll see later, cheaper accommodation in Spain doesn't always mean worse accommodation.

After a short siesta, we took a stroll round the town which contained quite a few upmarket boutiques and tourist shops that all seemed to sell quality stuff as opposed to the usual tourist tat. We heard quite a few people speaking French, and I guess that, with the French border only being around 40 kilometres (25 miles) away, this area must be a popular destination with the French as well as the Spanish.

Having spent several years learning Spanish after buying our apartment in Spain, our Spanish is good enough for us to have basic conversations, but although people seemed to understand us OK, we could make absolutely no sense of some of the locals when they replied. It suddenly dawned on us that we were now in Catalonia, where they speak Catalan and not Castilian Spanish. We try not to be like many Brits who move to Spain and expect the Spanish to speak English, so we make a point of doing our best to speak Spanish when we're speaking to Spanish people. In fact, we've had some good fun doing this, and especially because the Spanish always seem to appreciate our efforts, even if making sense has sometimes been a bit of a trial for all of us. It's also quite common to have conversations where, even though we're speaking in Spanish, Spanish people insist on speaking to us in English, presumably to help us or to make us feel more comfortable. Imagine someone in the UK acting like that with a foreigner when they walk into a shop and need some assistance. I remembered the Catalonians consider themselves to be an autonomous part of Spain and have been making moves to become independent. Catalonia later declared independence with quite dramatic results.

The locals in question could understand our Spanish, so why didn't they reply to us in the same language? Maybe they were just making the point that we were in Catalonia, but I did find this to be unlike our usual experiences when we practised our language skills in other parts of Spain or, at least, in Spanish Spain. Maybe the French, who, as many Brits know, make a point of not speaking any other language than their own, were having an influence?

We eventually settled on a good restaurant overlooking the bay, where our waitress chatted away to us in "proper" Spanish, and we enjoyed a leisurely dinner. We finished the day off with a bottle of red in a beach bar before retiring to our hotel for a reasonably early night.

On the road to Cadaqués

14

Day 11, 17 May

Route: Cadaqués — Cap de Creus — Cadaqués
Distance today: 17 kilometres (11 miles)
Distance so far: 1,879 kilometres (1,168 miles)
Bike Time: 1 hour 30 minutes
Overnight: Hostal Marina, Cadaqués

When we went down to breakfast in the Hostal Marina, we were told there wasn't any because it was a holiday. We'd blagged the last room in the hotel, so it was obviously full of guests, most likely because of the public holiday itself, yet there was no breakfast. Seemingly, the hotel staff are allowed to take public holidays, too, which is a bit strange when you consider that hotels are likely to be quite busy during holiday periods. This is Spain, so we find it hard to get annoyed about these things; it's just part of living there, and we make allowances because the many good things about Spain are a fair trade-off for what would be frustrations anywhere else. Queues, for example.

I hate queuing, and in the bank or the post office in Spain, there's almost always a queue. The tellers are sometimes efficient and sometimes a bit slow, and there's usually an annoying person who keeps remembering they need something else each time you think they're about to conclude their transactions and leave. The tellers are generally friendly, however, and pass the time of day, discussing the customer's family or their latest hospital visits and they share a bit of gossip about what's going on in the town. Now, if I were anywhere else, I would be standing in the queue with steam coming out of my ears or wanting to point out at the top of my voice that they should get a bloody move on because there's a bloody queue. In Spain, however, I practise my Spanish by eavesdropping and trying to understand the conversation, and when I get to the front of the queue, I want to tell the cashier how my family are doing, about any aches and pains I might have and swap a bit of local gossip. You see, it's different here.

After moaning to Kim about the hotel not having any breakfast, I soon found out that, in truth, it wasn't much of an inconvenience because the staff at the beach restaurant across the street weren't on holiday, and it was consequently open for business. Having no particular plans for the day, we had a leisurely breakfast and a couple of cups of coffee whilst idly watching the boats in the bay going about their business. It made a pleasant change to have nothing much on the day's agenda. We'd now been on the road for eleven days, and so far, the trip had been pretty much full-on. We'd ridden around 1,800 kilometres (1,140 miles), which is about the same distance as from London to Rome, or New York to Miami, but looking at the map, we hadn't reached the halfway point of our circumnavigation.

Whilst we really wanted to do the whole route, we agreed there was no point in us busting a gut to do so if that meant we weren't enjoying ourselves. If push came to shove, we could always make a beeline for home from wherever we happened to be if we were to decide that time was against us. Anyway, today was to be a day off to allow us to recharge our batteries a little. Kim announced she wanted to do some laundry, and I needed to catch up on emails and call the office to see what was going on, but apart from that, the day was ours to do whatever took our fancy.

A couple of hours later, I'd done what I needed to do, and Kim was still pottering round the room — she always enjoys a good potter.

'How about we head off and do the Furthest Point this afternoon so we can hit the road to Andorra straight away in the morning?' I suggested.

'To be honest, I'd like a day off the bike. I'm quite happy chilling out here, but why don't you go?'

It was a nice day again — sunny with patchy clouds — and I quite fancied a bit of a burble on my own and without the luggage. (I was going to say "baggage", but Kim might take this the wrong way.) I'd been wondering whether the fact that the bike was fully loaded had anything to do with my horrible ride over the mountain the day before, so I welcomed the chance to test the theory and started to change out of my T-shirt and shorts and into my riding gear.

Spain's Furthest Point East is at Cap de Creus which can be found at the point of a short, fat peninsula. It's just a short distance along the coast from Cadaqués, but the road linking the two places twists its way over the top of the rocky and hilly promontory. Heading out of Cadaqués, the signposts to Cap de Creus directed me to make a turn onto a very narrow and very bumpy road. An adventure bike with longer and softer suspension to soak up the bumps would probably have been more suitable than a large touring bike, but I was in no particular hurry and took it easy so that I could enjoy the quite spectacular moorland scenery under the sunny skies.

The road was so narrow that it was necessary to slow down when approaching oncoming traffic. I spotted a new-looking 3-series BMW convertible approaching with the top down, and as we passed each other, I noticed that the driver had, as my old gran used to say, "a face as long as Norfolk Street." I attempted to catch his eye and wish him good morning, but he looked straight ahead and steadfastly ignored me. I thought it was a shame that he didn't seem to be enjoying the beautiful day and the spectacular surroundings whilst in his rather nice car.

A little further down the road, I spotted a Morgan, and as we approached each other, the driver and I gave each other a big grin and a cheery wave and, as we passed alongside, exchanged greetings.

In direct contrast to Señor Misery-Guts BMW Driver, the guy in the Morgan knew what it was all about, and I'm sure he and his lady companion would have had a thoroughly enjoyable day.

As the road approached Cap de Creus, I could see in the distance that the Furthest Point East was marked by a lighthouse and a couple of buildings. Hopefully, one of them would be a café where I could get a cup of coffee and a bun. The road eventually deposited me in a car park, so I parked Roadie and had a stroll round the tops of the cliffs of the rocky headland, watched the waves smash on the rock far below and noticed quite a few ships sailing along the Mediterranean. There's something a little mystical about these extreme points, and as I stood there, I realised that, if the crow flew directly east from there, the next dry land he would find would be Corsica, and from there, it would be just another short flight to Italy. I hoped the crow had strong wings because it would be quite a flight.

There was, indeed, a restaurant, and I grabbed an outside table and enjoyed my coffee and pastry in the sun. The Spanish-French border was only a few kilometres away, and as I looked towards the north, I wondered exactly where along the coastline Spain finished and France began. After thinking about the crow, I idly speculated how long it would take us to get to Italy via France from our home in Portugal, although that would have to be done on another trip because this one was dedicated to the Furthest Points.

Coffee and pastry consumed, I fired up Roadie and parked her in front of a monument which marked the spot as being the Furthest Point East and, in my best Spanish, asked a couple who were passing by to take a couple of photos of us in front of the obelisk in order to record the occasion for posterity. They said they would be pleased to. They actually said, 'Nous serions heureux de prendre votre photo,' which indicated they were French but had, nevertheless, managed to understand my Spanish. Photos taken and camera stowed away, I set off back on the road to Cadaqués and, along the way, exchanged cheery waves with a couple of guys out for a ride on their classic bikes. Another couple of guys who got it.

It's been many years since I've owned a classic bike. Well, to be more precise, in those days it was really more of an old bike than a classic, and I only owned twenty-five per cent of it. Let me explain.

When I was fourteen, a couple of my schoolmates had spotted an old bike in the back of a garage at a house which was on their way to school. One day, they knocked on the door and asked if it might be for sale. It was, and the upshot was that four of us each contributed a quarter of the price, which was .... wait for it .... the princely sum of two pounds. That's right! An investment of ten shillings from my paper-round money got me into classic bike ownership. On the day of the sale, Hoppy, Dave, Cardy and I paid the money to the owner and pushed the bike to Hoppy's house, where it was installed in his dad's garage. It was a Panther 650 single, known as a "sloper", because the singe cylinder was so long it had to be slanted at a forty-degree angle to keep the top rail of the frame at a sensible height. The engine formed a stressed member of the frame and acted in place of the more conventional front downtube.

Doing a bit of research for this book, I found that the heavyweight, single-cylindered engine was often described as firing "once every lamp post" due to the heavy flywheel and low rpm. I also discovered that Panthers were manufactured between 1904 and 1967 in Cleckheaton, Yorkshire, by Phelon & Moore. The end of production came, as it did for the rest of the British motorcycle industry, with the advent of affordable cars and more modern and cheaper Japanese bikes. Of course, we didn't know any of this. To us kids, it was just a bike, and we were dying to ride it.

Hoppy's dad, Doug, was a mechanic of some type and helped us to get it running and also showed us what the various controls were for, including a decompression lever to help when starting it with the kickstart. I remember it was a vicious beast, and if you weren't careful, it would kick back at you with very painful consequences. Possibly, working on the bike wasn't only the start of a lifelong love of motorcycles but also a lifelong love of tinkering with stuff, which as everyone knows, is a pastime which involves taking things to pieces and then trying to get them back together without having too many bits left over at the end of the operation.

I enjoyed working with Doug and took a keen interest as he showed us what various tools were used for and how to use them properly as we worked through the bike, checking and adjusting things and making sure everything worked properly. Eventually, the bike got Doug's stamp of approval, and we were ready to ride, so bearing in mind we didn't have driving licences and the bike wasn't taxed, tested or insured, we pushed it down the road to the "rec" or, to use its official title, the recreation ground. I'm not sure what type of recreation Sheffield City Council envisaged for this area when it was designated as a place for the recreation of the local population, because it just consisted of a large, bare field with four goalposts standing forlornly at either end of what, had there been any markings, could have been two football pitches, and that was it. No swings, no roundabouts and no slides, but that day, it did have a Panther motorcycle for our personal recreation.

I don't remember who was brave enough to take the first ride, but we eventually mastered the art of letting the clutch out slowly at the same time as winding on the gas to make it go. Presumably, we also worked out how to make it stop, unlike the mum of a friend of mine who went for a ride on her son's bike and had to keep going round the block because she didn't know how to stop it. After a while, we even managed to change gear as we wobbled our way round. That was it! I was hooked! I loved riding that bike, and for the next few weeks, I couldn't wait to get round to Hoppy's place and take the bike for a spin. Unfortunately, the people whose houses backed onto the rec didn't have the same love of bikes as we did, because one day,

Day 11, 17 May • 125

when Hoppy and I were riding round, a police car pulled onto the field and made a beeline for us.

'Hop on,' yelled Hoppy as he kicked the bike over and got on board. I jumped on the back, and he gunned the bike towards the other end of the rec where there was a rough path that led over a small stream onto some waste ground; a route the police car couldn't follow. Feeling like Steve McQueen in *The Great Escape*, we skidded and bounced our way to the road that led to Switzerland, errr, sorry, Hoppy's parents' house, where we quickly closed the garage doors to hide the bike from the Gestapo, sorry, police. We reckoned that the quisling neighbours, who were probably getting a bit annoyed at the sound of a loud motorcycle at the bottom of their gardens, had informed on us. We resolved to make repatriations after the war had ended.

Being young and stupid, this incident didn't deter us, and we continued to ride round the rec. It didn't deter the police either, because they kept coming back. On one occasion, I was on the bike and spotted the police driving into the field. I was heading for our escape route when I noticed a second police car heading to block us off. I thought I could get the bike up and over a steep bank, so after collecting Hoppy, I headed straight for it. Hoppy fell off the back about halfway up the bank, but I managed to get to the top. Hoppy scrambled up and jumped back on, and we were soon back in the garage, having evaded arrest once again.

The appeal of riding round in circles at the rec soon wore off, however, and we also realised it would only be a matter of time before Sheffield's finest managed to catch us. We had the brainwave that it would be a lot more fun if we rode the Panther on the road rather than the rec. We had to wait until Hoppy's mum and dad were out, of course, but as they were both at work all day, this wasn't much of a problem in the school holidays. We took to the local housing estates and eventually further afield and, for a few weeks, had a great time, showing off to our mates and trying to persuade girls to come for a ride. The fact that we had no road sense and knew nothing about the Highway Code didn't bother us at all, and neither did the fact that we were riding totally illegally. Until Hoppy got caught, that is.

Hoppy was out riding on his own one day when a police car started to follow him. He remembered that all we needed to do in such situations was to take the bike where the police car couldn't follow, so he swerved off the road, over the pavement and into a gennel (which, in Sheffield, is what we call a footpath that's used as a short-cut between adjacent roads) and made his escape. Only he didn't. As he rounded a corner on his way home, the police were coming the other way and, spotting their adversary, blocked the road with the car. This time there was no handy gennel, and the two policemen jumped out of the car and then jumped on Hoppy. The upshot of this was that Hoppy was arrested for riding without a licence and riding a motorcycle without tax, insurance or an MOT. He did, however, gain a lot of kudos amongst our mates for getting endorsements on his licence before he was even old enough to apply for one. The police dropped the resisting-arrest charge, though. I suppose two burly coppers would have looked a bit daft trying to get that one to stick against a fourteen-year-old.

The more serious consequence, however, was that our parents all took a dim view of our motorcycle escapades, and we were promptly ordered to get rid of the Panther. By this time, I'd well and truly been bitten by the motorcycling bug, and I decided all I needed to do was bide my time until I was sixteen, which in those days was the age that you could get a licence, and then I would be back on the road, with the added advantage that I would even be able to do so legally.

Many years later, when we were living in Dubai, I was at the annual Dubai Bike Show, where there was a section devoted to classic bikes. This being Dubai, where everything has to be the biggest and best and you must have the very latest model of everything, classic anything at all tends to be regarded as just being old and therefore rubbish. Consequently, the Classic Bike section was very small, with only about four bikes on display, but one of them was a Panther 650. It was by no means a show bike, and it looked distinctly tatty in some areas. As I was taking a few photos for nostalgia's sake, the English owner strolled up, and we started chatting. I explained I'd had this same model as my first bike (well, twenty-five per cent of it, anyway). He told me his father had bought this bike new in the 1950s, and after he stopped using it, it had lain unused in his garage for many years. After his father died, he decided to take the bike and make it roadworthy again. He, too, thought that originality was better than restoration so stopped short of powder-coating, repainting and re-chroming everything and just did what was necessary to make sure that the bike went, stopped, steered and was as reliable as an old British bike could ever be. I liked this concept, and I also thought that the fact that the bike had been bought new by his father and had spent more than fifty years in the ownership of father and son was really rather special. Somehow, a shiny restoration just wouldn't have been right.

A couple of hours later on my way home, I caught up with the guy puttering along the road on his Panther at a steady speed. I pulled alongside him, and we rode together for a while until I got bored of riding at classic bike speed, being overtaken by trucks and buses, and with a wave and a grin, I wound on the gas and headed for home. A nice guy with an interesting story.

Back at the hotel, I found Kim sunning herself on the balcony. It's probably obvious by now that the reason it was sunny was because this was a non-riding day. Kim was also multi-tasking by checking accommodation for our next stop in Andorra. I had a look at the map to work out a possible route after Andorra and noticed that all the roads seemed to go north-south, whereas we needed to go from the east to the west. This might prove to be a bit of a challenge unless we wanted to ride a route shaped like a paperclip. Ah, well, we would be sure to work something out when the time came.

I spent the rest of the afternoon taking a siesta and reading. When evening came round, neither of us could be bothered to get showered and changed to go out for dinner, so Kim nipped off to the supermarket and came back with a salad and a bottle of wine which we shared on the balcony. We agreed we'd thoroughly enjoyed our chillaxed day, and that it had made a welcome change. Another thing which made me cheer up was that Kim (remember, she is a Yorkshire woman and knows the value of a pound) had worked out that all our food and drink for the day had come to the grand total of €28.

We had now knocked off two Furthest Points, but we weren't even halfway round our route. Tomorrow, however, we would be heading for Andorra, an entirely new country.

Furthest Point East, Cap de Creus

Day 12, 18 May

Route: Cadaqués — Figueres — Olot — Ripoll — La Seu D'Urgell — Ordino
Distance today: 248 kilometres (154 miles)
Distance so far: 2,127 kilometres (1,322 miles)
Bike time: 6 hours 45 minutes
Overnight: Hotel Coma, Ordino, Andorra

By Day 12, we'd expended around sixty per cent of our allotted time for the trip, but by my reckoning, we'd only covered around forty per cent of our planned route. We needed to think about getting a bit of a wiggle on in the coming days. Well, today would be one such opportunity and wouldn't be difficult, provided the roads allowed us to maintain a decent speed, because our destination was Andorra. Looking at the map, we had two choices — the motorway route which would be around 300 kilometres (186 miles) or the A-road route which would be shorter and probably more fun but would undoubtedly take longer. Weighing up the options, I chose the fun route via Olot and Ripoll.

After our relaxing day the day before, we were up at seven thirty and on the road by eight fifteen and, as usual, we were setting off under overcast skies. It seemed that the only road out of Cadaqués was the narrow, windy mountain road on which we'd entered. This time it felt much better so, hopefully, whatever had caused my lack of confidence a couple of days before had passed. Exiting Figueres, the first sizeable town along the route, we found ourselves on a good A-road and travelling through greenery in gorgeous countryside from which we could see the Pyrenees in the distance, rising majestically towards the clouds. The sun had even broken through the early morning cloud cover and was brightening up the sky. A good road, lovely scenery, not much traffic and lovely weather — this was biker heaven.

After an hour or so in the saddle, we were ready for coffee and some breakfast, so I started looking for a likely place. This was a quiet rural area, so it took some time before I spotted a sign indicating there was a restaurant and a gas station off to the left. After several kilometres following a minor road through farmland, I began to wonder if the guy who'd put the sign up was having a laugh, but eventually, we arrived at a small industrial estate in the middle of nowhere. In Spain, wherever there are people, there's always somewhere selling food and drink, and we soon found a busy restaurant with views towards the distant mountains.

Fortified by caffeine and our mid-morning snack, we headed back to the A-road and soon found ourselves in Ripoll, where Satnav Woman guided us to a not very A-road-looking route out of town. *What the hell*, I thought. *Let's follow it anyway.* This was a good decision, because this narrow, winding B-road took us over the Coll de Merolla and through some spectacular scenery with views over lakes and mountains and down into deep valleys and gorges as we followed the twisty route. It was also a very, very long road which consisted almost entirely of slow-speed bends connected by very short straights, so I was in second or third gear almost all the way. Large, heavy touring bikes aren't exactly built for this type of road, and after a while, my arms were aching because they were pumped up from constantly operating the clutch and brake and the tension caused by setting up Roadie for each bend and then guiding her round, only to find there was another bend almost immediately in front of us.

I eventually pulled off the road to take a break, and apart from the ticking of Roadie's engine as it cooled down, there was almost total silence. We'd hardly seen any other vehicles on this road, and we'd passed almost no signs of habitation. It was reminiscent of some of the areas we'd ridden through in the United States, and it felt as though we were alone in a vast wilderness. We smiled at each other and had a hug, each knowing how much we both love this type of place.

Back on the bike, it was more of the same for many kilometres, and I was pretty tired when we re-joined an A-road and got some relief from the constant gear changing and braking. What a fantastic road! What an experience! Yes, I'd ridden roads like it before but never over such a long distance, and what little of the scenery I'd been able to see, whilst taking my eyes off the road for a second or two, was magnificent.

I have to take a moment here to sing the praises of Kim, who is an amazingly good motorcycle passenger. In fact, riding with Kim is just the same as riding with no Kim. In other words, I don't really notice she's there. If you think that being a good passenger on a motorcycle is easy, it isn't. A bad passenger is hard work for the rider. Kim leans with the bike at exactly the right time and uses her own body language to help me balance when we're moving at walking pace in heavy traffic. She's totally comfortable on the back of a bike, and I've even known her fall asleep on a few occasions. I notice this when I feel her helmet bump against the back of my own. She's never once told me to slow down or had a go at me for anything, even after some enthusiastic footboard-scraping along roads such as the one we'd just travelled.

Given how good she is on a motorcycle, it's totally weird that she's completely the opposite when in a car. I enjoy my cars as much as my bikes, and I've had some nice vehicles in my time, some of which have been rather quick. Phrases such as 'You're going far too fast!' 'Watch that truck!' and 'For God's sake, slow down!' are often accompanied by Kim flinching violently in the passenger seat when I'm enjoying myself. I've consequently learned that the time to enjoy, shall we say, spirited driving is when Kim isn't with me.

Back on less challenging roads, the route followed a wide and turbulent river, and at one point, we rode through a 5-kilometre (3-mile) tunnel. I'm not keen on tunnels for some reason. Maybe it's the fact it's too dark to see if I keep my sunglasses on, and the wind makes my eyes water if I take them off, plus I can't see too well with them off anyway because, these days, I need prescription glasses for riding and driving. Maybe it's the feeling of tunnel vision that I get (no pun intended) and the disorientation that comes from the lack of spatial awareness caused by not being able to judge your speed very well because there are no natural reference points to go by.

We stopped for lunch at a picturesque little town and found a restaurant beside the river which runs alongside the main street. We took an outside table from which we had still more views into the Pyrenees which were where we were headed and which were significantly closer by now. Whilst we were relaxing over our coffees, a guy rode past on a Harley with his lady sitting in a sidecar. They must have spotted Roadie parked in front of the restaurant and Kim and I still in our biker gear so gave us a wave and a smile as they burbled past.

One of my earliest memories is being in my dad's sidecar wearing rubber swimming goggles and standing on the seat with my head poking up through the canvas roof. I also remember travelling to my gran and grandad's caravan at Skegness with Mom sitting on the back of the bike and me in the sidecar surrounded by luggage and provisions for our holiday. (Eating out wasn't an option in those days, and Mom took all our food with us in tins.) I must have only been about three or four at the time, and the sidecar was one of those fully enclosed ones with a roll-back canvas roof. Maybe this early memory is another reason why I like convertible cars.

Another memory from round the same time was sitting on the tank of my dad's ex-Post Office BSA Bantam as he rode round the fields at the back of our house, which were soon to have semi-detached houses built on them and become part of the new suburban housing estate we'd just moved onto. In the days before owning a telephone was commonplace, the General Post Office used Bantams for the delivery of telegrams, and Dad's was still in its red Post Office livery. I must have got the biker bug fairly early because I remember thinking it would be great to be a telegram boy and have your own red motorcycle. I even remember Mom telling me that being a telegram boy wasn't much of a career and that I should set my sights a bit higher. Taking her advice, I considered becoming an AA or RAC patrol man because, in those days, they had bikes too.

Maybe biking is just part of my genes because my grandad was also a biker. He was a military policeman in the Second World War, and I once had a photo of him astride a motorcycle in the North African desert, looking very smart in his uniform. I wish I still had that photo. When I was young, my dad at various times had the Bantam, a Triumph, which I think could have been a Thunderbird, and an Aerial. Motorcycles were more of a cheap form of transport in those days because only well-off people could aspire to car ownership. Dad must have been a biker at heart because, when he was in his fifties, he became a born-again biker, starting with a Honda step-through and then graduating to a Honda 250 Superdream and, eventually, to a BMW R65. At that time, I had two young children and didn't have a bike of my own, but I regularly used to borrow one of Dad's bikes for a blast into the nearby Derbyshire Peak District and once took the BMW to Snowdonia for a weekend. And, yes, such was my love of being on two wheels again, I even borrowed the step-through on some occasions.

Back on Roadie, our destination for the night was only 57 kilometres (35 miles) away, and we set off along another agreeably windy A-road towards La Seu d'Urgell, after which we would head north into Andorra. As we rode along, I noticed the skies were black in the north and seemed to be getting blacker every time I looked. Ever the optimist, I hoped the rain would either not manifest itself or that we would make it to our destination before it started. Optimist I may be, but meteorologist I'm not, so consequently, we weren't wearing our waterproofs when the heavens opened about 20 kilometres (12 miles) from our destination. I managed to stop in a short tunnel so we could put our wets on without getting any wetter. When we emerged, we found that just round the corner was the Andorran border. What little we saw of Andorra La Vella, as we rode through the streaming rain, was through misted-up glasses and visors.

What we did see, however, seemed to consist of lots of duty-free shopping outlets and blocks of apartments. Kim hadn't fancied Andorra La Vella when she was researching places to stay and had booked us into a hotel in Ordino, 15 kilometres (9 miles) to the north. These last kilometres seemed to take forever because the rain was still bucketing it down, and it was quite a busy road, so it was hard to make quick progress. After such a great day's riding, the rain hadn't dampened our spirits because we both managed a laugh at the fact that, just as we arrived at Hotel Coma, it stopped raining, and the sun came out.

Hotel Coma was constructed from natural pine and stone and looked very alpine with its ornately carved shutters, balustraded balconies and steeply pitched roof. The Swiss chalet theme was repeated inside, and although the furnishing and décor looked a little time-worn, it seemed like a comfortable place to stay. It was also a welcoming place because the receptionist made a big fuss of us, asking where we'd ridden from and where we were going and seemed very interested in our journey. She also offered the hotel's private basement garage for me to park Roadie for the night.

Andorra is an independent, Catalan-speaking principality located amongst the southern peaks of the Pyrenees and has a distinctly alpine feel about it. Although it's not part of the European Union, it uses the Euro as its currency, and its tax rates are either zero or very low, and this, together with tourism, firstly in summer and then winter when skiing takes place, seems to provide its principal source of business. The principality has an area of only 468 square kilometres (191 square miles), which makes it just a little larger than England's smallest two counties of Rutland and the Isle of Wight. It has a population of only 77,000 which is around the same as Tamworth or Fylde in England. The fact I've no clue where either Tamworth or Fylde are just goes to show that Andorra doesn't have a very big population. To sum up, then, Andorra isn't very big and doesn't have a large population, but it's very pretty when it's not throwing it down.

We thought we deserved a quick drink before repairing to our room. Whilst the bartender was serving us, he advised that the weather had been absolutely awful that year, the economy was in a bad state, business was bad, his gout was giving him gyp, and global warming would be the death of us all within a year or two. He wasn't exactly a glass-half-full type! As we sat at the bar, the adjoining room began to fill with new arrivals, and we heard several cut-glass English accents from the well-dressed and mainly elderly clientele. The barman explained there was about to be a musical soirée, and the local British cultural society had turned out in force to listen. Despite the fact we hadn't heard any English spoken by a native since we'd left Barcelona, we didn't feel inclined to make conversation. After all, we couldn't imagine what these posh, grey-haired tax exiles would have in common with a couple of damp, Northern bikers. One lady from the group did, however, make a beeline for us and said hello in accented Spanish. She'd noticed our Harley clothes and had come over to tell us she was from Germany and rode a Harley Sportster. I wonder if she ever revealed this snippet to the rest of the cultural society. The music — a piano recital of some sort — commenced, and we retired to our room to unpack and relax for an hour or two before dinner.

The room was decorated and furnished in a similar style to the rest of the hotel with a lot of bare pine. It also had spectacular views from the balcony that included a couple of ski runs with their cable cars standing forlornly whilst waiting for the next snows to come.

Later, showered and changed, we wandered down and stuck our heads through the dining room door to check it out. Not much liking what we saw (more pine), we headed to the village to check out the action there. Ordino is a charming little place, but it was a little quiet. Maybe the summer season hadn't kicked in yet, but there wasn't a lot open and not much going on, so after a quick mooch round, we chose one of the few restaurants that were open and tucked into some very tasty tapas, cooked and served by the owner / waiter / bartender / chef who explained he'd only opened the restaurant a couple of months ago. He was a happy, friendly guy. The food was great, and he looked after us very well, so I hoped his new venture would be a great success. We also decided that Mr Miserable Bartender could have taken a leaf out of his book.

Mr Miserable Bartender was still on duty when we returned to the hotel for a nightcap. Whilst he hadn't cheered up in the intervening few hours, he at least made my night when I ordered a glass of Glenlivet, and he poured me an enormous measure together with a similar-sized brandy for Kim. Our glasses were definitely half full that night. When we'd finished our very large snifters and were ready to settle the bill and go to our room, he'd completely disappeared. I wandered round the hotel looking for him so that I could pay, but without success, so I explained the situation to the receptionist and requested her to ask him to put the drinks on our room bill so that we could pay when we checked out.

The central heating in our room seemed to be set for the ski season, and it was oppressively hot and stuffy, so I opened the window to let in some fresh air before getting into bed. That day we'd covered 248 kilometres (154 miles) and had been in the saddle for almost seven hours. We'd ridden some wonderful, if challenging, roads and had travelled through magnificent countryside, not to mention a 5-kilometre (3-mile) tunnel. We'd also been warmed by the sun and soaked by torrential rain. No wonder I didn't take much rocking and immediately fell into a deep sleep.

The road to Andorra

16

Day 13, 19 May

Route: Andorra — Lleida — Huesca — Ayerbe — Loarre
Distance today: 316 kilometres (196 miles)
Distance so far: 2,443 kilometres (1,518 miles)
Bike time: 5 hours 30 minutes
Overnight: El Callejon de Andrese Hotel, Loarre

I woke at eight o'clock and, looking over to Kim, noticed she had a face like a smacked bum. 'Morning, honey. How are you? Did you sleep OK?' I enquired, already suspecting the answer wasn't going to be very positive, and it would probably be all my fault.

'No. I didn't! *Somebody* left the window open last night, and there are pollen trees right outside, so I woke up in the middle of the night sneezing, and my eyes were streaming.'

I knew it would be all my fault.

We got dressed and packed in that stony silence that husbands know so well and which means "I'm going to make you suffer for quite a while yet for being such a dick." Women have a way of doing accusatory silence in a way that's totally different to just being quiet. Maybe it's just the Venusian genes?

After we'd lugged the bags downstairs, Kim broke the silence by announcing that the hotel breakfast was too expensive, so we wouldn't be having anything. She was probably just trying to make me suffer for a while longer, but she did have a point. Hotel breakfast policies are something else I find annoying. It's not that I'm tight-fisted about such things. I'm not, but my usual breakfast consists of a cup of coffee, a couple of slices of toast or a bowl of muesli and a couple of cigarettes. Whilst I realise that the average hotel buffet breakfast allows you to munch yourself through several courses, I don't want to do that. I don't see why I should alter my eating habits and gorge myself just to get value for money.

Having mounted and started the bike, I realised that I'd forgotten to put my earplugs in, so I had to get off, remove my helmet and insert them. Going for a bike ride is very different to going out in a car. This is what happens when I go anywhere in my car:

Approach car with keyless entry fob in pocket;
Open car door which has automatically unlocked itself;
Get inside;
Close door;
Put foot on brake pedal;
Press start;
Fasten seat belt;
Engage drive;
Release hand brake;
Press accelerator and go.

An easy, ten-step process which takes about ten seconds.

And now for the bike, and this is after I've already changed into my riding gear:

Approach bike, carrying helmet and gloves;
Hang helmet on mirror;

Put gloves on saddle;
Unlock steering lock;
Unlock ignition switch;
Put keys in jeans pocket;
Remove keys from jeans pocket because, when I'm riding, they'll end up sticking in my leg;
Put keys in jacket pocket;
Zip up jacket pocket so I don't lose keys;
Zip up bike jacket;
Fasten bike jacket cuffs;
Put on and fasten helmet;
Pick up gloves from floor where they ended up after sliding off saddle;
Put on gloves and tighten Velcro straps;
Get on bike;
Raise kickstand;
Check the bike is in neutral;
Turn on ignition;
Press start;
Realise it's rather loud, so I must have forgotten my earplugs;
Turn off bike;
Lower kickstand;
Get off bike;
Remove gloves and place them on saddle;
Unzip jacket pocket and remove key;
Unlock and open saddlebag;
Retrieve earplugs;
Close and lock saddlebag;
Return keys to jacket pocket and ensure it's zipped;
Remove helmet and hang it on mirror;
Insert earplugs;
Put on and fasten helmet;
Pick up gloves from floor where they ended up after sliding off saddle again;
Put on gloves and fasten Velcro;

Get back on bike;
Raise kickstand;
Check bike is still in neutral;
Turn on ignition;
Press start;
Pull in clutch lever;
Engage first gear;
Apply gas, release clutch and go.

A forty-two-step process that takes about half an hour. You'll appreciate that, if I'm popping out for a bottle of milk, I usually take the car. Come to think of it, walking would be quicker than going by bike.

We were on the road by nine thirty. It was very cool, so we needed several layers, but it was a lovely, sunny day. As we headed through Andorra La Vella en route back to Spain, we spotted a Harley-Davidson shop and stopped for a mooch round. Kim spotted a stylish waterproof jacket and promptly decided her old one was past its best (it actually was), so I could buy her this one as a replacement. Mindful of the fact I wasn't quite out of the dog house for the pollen-tree incident, I coughed up €380. I remember thinking that, at that price, I hoped it would rain for the rest of the trip so we'd get good value for money out of it. Maybe now she would let me have some breakfast before too long. Come to think of it, how come she who thought the price of a €15 breakfast was too much but didn't blink an eye at €380 for a jacket? Venusian logic at work again, I suppose.

Our next way-point was to be Lleida which was about two hours to the south-west. At first, the road took us alongside mountains covered in green pines, through tunnels and beside lakes — another great road with gorgeous scenery. We stopped in the sunny town square at Ponts for coffee and a pastry which served as a well-overdue breakfast. It was getting hot now, so we layered off, hoping the weather would remain the same for the rest of the day. We mounted up and headed down the road, eventually leaving the mountains behind, and as we approached Lleida, into some rolling hills followed by flatter lands with wide horizons. From Lleida, we headed northwest towards Huesca and found ourselves travelling along another picturesque route, consisting of a motorway interspersed with good A-roads. Roadie was burbling away beneath us as reliably as ever, and it dawned on me that the new seat had proved to be an excellent investment because I hadn't once had a numb bum on the whole trip.

As we rode along the A-132 from Huesca towards Ayerbe, the pleasant ride we'd been having so far became hard work thanks to a very strong, gusty wind, and I began to feel uncomfortable with my riding again. I still couldn't work out where this feeling kept coming from. *Maybe this should be my last big trip. Maybe we should have done it in the car.* I wasn't in a good riding vibe at all and didn't welcome such negative thoughts which went against my whole biker ethos.

We turned off the A-132 at Ayerbe into country lanes towards Loarre, which was to be our destination for the night, and were being blown from one side of the narrow lane to the other. Eventually, we arrived safe and sound without being blown into a roadside ditch. Loarre is a small, rustic village with very narrow, cobbled streets which have the original drainage channels running down their centres. Satnav Woman had been programmed with the street name for our overnight stay but was throwing a wobbler and directing us in one direction or another and then immediately changing her mind. We couldn't find the guesthouse, so I returned to the village plaza and asked three elderly locals, who were sitting gossiping, for directions. 'Hola. ¿Donde está el Callejon del Andrese Hotel?' (Hello. Where is the Callejon del Andrese Hotel?)

They immediately all started talking at once and pointing in different directions. After a minute or two listening to them arguing amongst themselves and making no sense of anything they were saying, I decided it was a forlorn cause and, with a quick *'Gracias, hasta luego'* (thanks, see you later), jumped back on the bike. Four roads were leading out of what appeared to be the central plaza. We'd arrived on one of them and saw no sign of our hotel, so that left three possibilities, and I would explore each of them in turn. The first street was blocked, so I had to do a three-point turn and return to the square. The second took us out of the village with no hotel in view along the way, and the third, after many tight turns in the narrow streets, eventually led us to the guesthouse.

So far on this trip, we'd stayed in a variety of places. The parador in Lorca; Yasmin and David's villa in Denia; the boutique hotel in Peñíscola; the modern, four-star hotel in Barcelona; the fairly basic hotel in Cadaqués and the Swiss chalet-type hotel in Andorra. Calling the Callejon de Andrese Hotel a hotel was pushing it a bit because it was really a guesthouse. Having said that, it was a very charming guesthouse, and we loved it.

The proprietor was waiting to welcome us and proudly showed us round the very old, very rustic and quirkily decorated property. There were just four guest rooms, all individually and stylishly decorated, and a combined dining room-cum-lounge which had a beamed ceiling, stone floor and various antiques, curios and diverse collections of all sorts of things from photographic equipment to shaving paraphernalia. The owners must have spent a lot of time at antique fairs to have amassed all this stuff. I spotted a collection of old, Vespa scooter models and asked the proprietor if he liked scooters. He told me he liked both classic cars and classic motorcycles. We chatted about classic cars and found we both have a love for old Mercedes. He showed me photos of his 1965 250S, and not to be outdone, I got out my phone and showed him pictures of my 1994 SL320. We were obviously kindred spirits and could have continued to chat about bikes and cars, but another couple of guests arrived and needed his attention, so I took the bags up to the room that Kim had selected having been invited to choose which one she preferred.

After spending some time showering, snoozing and planning the next day's itinerary, we set off to the village to find somewhere for dinner, only to find that all the restaurants and cafés in the plaza were closed. Kim remembered seeing one place on the outskirts of the village, so with fingers crossed and rumbling stomachs, we set off to the Last Chance Saloon in the hope it would be open. We were eventually to become glad that the other places had been closed because, otherwise, we would probably not have walked the extra distance to find this place where the owner-cum-chef-cum-barman made us very welcome and served us simple but delicious meals, featuring local produce. When we lived in the Middle East, most of the "fresh" food was imported and had probably spent weeks being shipped before it reached the restaurant or supermarket and, as a result, usually didn't have much flavour. The vegetables we were eating that night had probably been growing in a field a couple of days before and my pork steak still in a sty. The marked difference in eating out in the two regions was also reinforced by the fact that our dinner would only cost about 20% of the equivalent, but less tasty, meal in Dubai.

We were just finishing our meal when the people who'd checked into the guesthouse just after us arrived and took the table next to us, and we soon started chatting. Debbie and Rob were from New Zealand. They were in the middle of a walking holiday and staying in rural guesthouses such as this one each night.

'That sounds like a great holiday,' I remarked. 'How long will it take?'

'Oh, eight weeks or thereabouts,' Rob replied casually.

'Bloody hell! I was expecting you to say something like a week or ten days. That's one hell of a trip.'

'Yeah. We did a similar thing a couple of years ago, but that time we camped. This time we don't have to carry the camping gear, so we're taking it a bit easier.'

Considering that Rob and Debbie were in their mid to late-sixties, I found this to be an incredible thing for them to be doing and began to feel a bit embarrassed about moaning about a bit of wind earlier on in the day — even though it was a very strong wind.

I've always wanted to spend some time in New Zealand and wondered why, when it contains so much natural beauty, Rob and Debbie felt the need to fly to the other side of the world to go hiking.

Debbie explained that New Zealand is so sparsely populated, the distances between places to stay are too far apart, so you have to camp and carry all your own provisions.

We ended up staying until quite late and had a lovely time chatting to our new-found friends. They were very interesting, great company and a remarkable couple. We shared a few bottles of wine, and the four of us were somewhat wobbly when we eventually made our way back to the guesthouse.

As I was dropping off to sleep, I remembered that, when I'd been planning our route that afternoon, I'd looked at the map of the Iberian Peninsula and, after noting our current position, had realised we still had a very long way to go. We were planning to ride along the Spanish North Atlantic Coast to the Furthest Point North and then to the Furthest Point West. I'd always thought the northern Atlantic coast of Spain was fairly short, but it isn't. From Irun on the French border in the east to A Coruña in the west is 663 kilometres (411 miles), which is the same distance as London to Edinburgh. Not only that, we still had around 300 kilometres (186 miles) to go before we even reached the coast.

To give you some idea of where we were on our trip, imagine the Iberian Peninsula as a clock, with Madrid roughly in the centre. Our home would be at the seven o'clock position, and we were currently at about two o'clock. Despite the fact we had so far ridden 2,443 kilometres (1,518 miles), or around the same distance as from London to Kiev, or Sydney to Cairns, we'd covered less than half of our planned route. By now we were two weeks into the trip, so we had used up two thirds of our time. I was beginning to have even stronger doubts as to whether we would be able to finish the whole trip.

El Callejon de Andrese Hotel, Loarre

17

Day 14, 20 May

Route: Loarre — Pamplona — Estella — Maeztu
Distance today: 243 kilometres (151 miles)
Distance so far: 2,686 kilometres (1,669 miles)
Bike time: 4 hours 30 minutes
Overnight: Hotel Rural los Roturos, Maeztu

Considering this was an old guesthouse full of rustic charm, our bathroom had a very modern and very complicated shower, which included three or four different places from which water was squirted. After spending some time attempting to fathom out the controls whilst being squirted from all directions with alternating scalding and freezing water, I eventually managed to take my morning shower. On arriving for breakfast, we found the proprietor was absent. Apparently, he also owned the village patisserie and had to open up at nine o'clock. He had, however, laid out a really good rustic breakfast (no doubt provided by the patisserie) for the guests to help themselves. Over breakfast, we chatted with a Spanish couple from Barcelona and, later, said our goodbyes to Debbie and Rob who were just setting off on the next leg of their marathon hike.

We both loved this guesthouse, and when I asked Kim what our night's stay had cost, I was pleasantly surprised to discover it was only €60 including breakfast. Kim knows from operating our apartment in Spain for holiday lets just how much work is required when guests check out. Towels and bed linen need to be changed and laundered, and everything has to be given a thorough clean in readiness for the next guests. As charming as it was, it didn't seem the sort of place people would book for more than a few days, because there was not a lot going on in the locality. This meant an almost constant turn-around and, consequently, a lot of cleaning and laundry. The proprietor was obviously not making a fortune from this business, but having chatted to him at length the day before, I got the feeling he just liked doing it, and after all, that's what life should be all about.

We were on the road at nine thirty, heading to our first way-point of Pamplona. The road was magnificent. We rode through a long gorge with the road clinging to mountains on one side and with a sheer drop on the other, down to a rushing river. This reminded both of us of the route we'd once ridden through the Yosemite National Park. We eventually exited the gorge and were met with a stunning vista displaying a calendar-type view of the snow-covered Pyrenees set beyond a wide plain. This was a must-stop photo opportunity, and after taking our pictures, we stayed for a while, just drinking in the wonderful view.

The wondrously curvy road then followed the shore of a strangely peppermint-green coloured lake for many kilometres. Today, I was back in the riding zone and was enjoying leaning Roadie over and piloting her through the numerous flowing bends. Hopefully, my mojo had returned.

We stopped for gas and, after filling up and riding round for a while, realised we must be in the only village in Spain without a café, so we were soon back on the road. We stopped again at around midday for coffee and a sausage sandwich on the outskirts of Pamplona where I programmed Satnav Woman for the next leg. This was to be along the A-12 motorway for 40 kilometres (25 miles), after which we would leave the motorway and follow an A-road for a further 40 kilometres (25 miles) to that day's destination of Maeztu. Not too far to go then!

This was the second time I'd visited Pamplona. On my earlier trip, however, I'd been riding solo from the UK to our apartment in Spain. This came about after we'd been using our new apartment for holidays for a couple of years and had decided a motorcycle would be a good thing to have in Spain to use whilst we were there. I subsequently bought a Harley Dyna from eBay and, after a flight from Dubai, jumped on it and, with no particular plan (does this sound familiar?), I rode it to Ayamonte, taking four days to do the trip by diverse routes through France and Spain. Revisiting Pamplona brought back many pleasant memories.

Satnav Woman took us on a convoluted tour of the back roads of Pamplona before spitting us out onto the ring road, where a newly constructed roundabout seemed to confuse her, and we ended up going the wrong way and having to make a U-turn.

Satnav Woman and I had enjoyed a love-hate relationship for a few years. I'd disdained the use of satnavs for some time because I've always had a love of maps; one that originated in my days as a Boy Scout and through a love of geography at school. We're very lucky in the UK to have such a wonderful institution as the Ordnance Survey whose maps are almost like works of art. I love poring over large-scale Ordnance Survey maps where individual buildings, post offices, churches (either with steeples or towers) are neatly shown over the topographical details of the landscape. With an Ordnance Survey map, you can accurately plan a hike or a drive down to the minutest detail, and you don't get that amount of entertainment from a small satnav screen.

I also like to get a general impression when looking for a good route between two points and, for this, it's also necessary to see the bigger picture. Even a decent road atlas will let you know whether the route is straight, bendy, travels through countryside or over mountains and what class of road you're likely to be travelling on.

One thing Ordnance Survey maps aren't very good for, however, is reading whilst on a motorcycle. They tend to get blown about a lot, so, in pre-Satnav Woman days, our usual method of getting from one place to another was to write the route down on a piece of paper so Kim could navigate and direct me along the way. This method of navigation isn't always perfect; for example, if you're trying to find a specific hotel in a strange town.

A few years earlier, Kim and I were riding to the Spanish Pyrenees on a rented Road King and had decided to spend a day exploring Bordeaux en route. We'd booked a hotel for a couple of nights, and Kim had the directions and a location map to hand as we entered Bordeaux. Travel being what it is, it's a typical scenario that you'll be entering an unfamiliar city during the late afternoon rush hour after a tiring day in the saddle. On this occasion, it was also very hot, and I was overheating in my riding gear in the slow, city traffic. We'd found the area in which the hotel was situated. In fact, we'd found the actual road, but it was a one-way street, and we couldn't find a route that reached the hotel from the right direction. After thirty minutes or so and several tours of central Bordeaux, with me becoming increasingly tired, uncomfortable and, according to Kim, bad tempered, I gave up and parked the Harley on a handy sidewalk, as close as we could get to the hotel, and we humped the luggage a couple of hundred metres to the next street and the hotel. I think this was the thin end of the wedge that culminated in my affair with Satnav Woman. I remember thinking at the time that it would have been much easier to have a satnav guide us to our destination in such situations.

Satnav Woman lives in a Garmin zūmo which is specially designed for bikes. The kit I bought contained a handlebar mount which is wired into the electrical system so that it stays permanently charged and can be quickly unclipped and slipped into a pocket when leaving the bike unattended. It also connects via Bluetooth to our helmet speakers so I can have two women telling me I've just made a wrong turn. A useful feature is that it contains another mount that can be fixed by a suction cup to a car windscreen, saving on yet another add-on that car rental companies try to get you to pay for.

The arrival of Satnav Woman was around the time we started to use the apartment we'd recently taken possession of in Spain and to explore the area. We soon found out that, unlike ebony and ivory, Spain and satnavs don't always live together in perfect harmony. Many of Spain's cities, towns and even villages date back to medieval times and, unlike the UK, where inner cities were demolished to make way for grand Victorian civic buildings and the like, they've remained pretty much as they were several hundreds of years ago. Imagine a Cornish fishing village with narrow cobbled streets laid out in a haphazard manner. Now, multiply the area of a Cornish fishing village by a factor of quite a few, and you'll begin to get the idea of a fairly typical Spanish town or city centre. I don't know how satnavs get their information, but something seems to be lacking in the information flow between the ancient Spanish road layouts and Satnav Command, which has led to a few interesting scenarios between me and Satnav Woman.

Satnav Woman: 'In one hundred metres, take the turning on the left.'

Me, making the turn: 'Thank you so much.'

Satnav Woman: 'Recalculating.'

Me: 'What?'

Satnav Woman: 'Recalculating.'

Me, slowing down and collecting a few cars behind me: 'Bloody hell, get a move on, will you! Where next?'

Satnav Woman: 'Recalculating.'

Car behind: 'Beep!'

Me: 'Piss off! I'm lost, and your Spanish road systems are useless.'

Satnav Woman: 'At the first opportunity, make a U-turn.'

Me: 'Have you seen the size of these streets? There's not enough room to swing a cat, let alone make a U-turn.'

Satnav Woman: 'Make a U-turn.'

Me: 'Bloody hell. Hang on a bit, will you? I'm trying to find a place to turn round.'

Satnav Woman: 'Make a U-turn.'

I eventually manage to negotiate a few streets, and we're heading back towards the original junction from the same direction as before.

Satnav Woman: 'In one hundred metres, take the next turning on the left.'

Me: 'I don't bloody believe it! You said that last time, you stupid woman, and then you immediately told me to make a bloody U-turn because it was the wrong bloody direction!'

Kim: 'There's a road sign there for where we want to go. Why don't you just go that way?'

Anyway, this brings me nicely back to the fact that Satnav Woman was apparently unaware of Pamplona's newish roundabout but did eventually manage to point us in the right direction.

Leaving the motorway after Pamplona, we followed the A-road through the countryside until we reached our rural hotel at Maeztu at a quarter to two, which was a nice early finish to the day's ride.

According to Kim-Dot-Com, the Hotel los Roturos is famous locally for its tapas, and, as the weather was perfect, we sat outside in our T-shirts to make the most of the sun and enjoyed a selection of their delicious tapas and drinks before retiring to our room for a siesta. As we dropped off to sleep, we listened to the village gossip from the locals sitting chattering away below the open bedroom window.

Before dinner, Kim spent an hour or so trying to find a hotel for the following day. This, however, turned out to be somewhat frustrating. Frustrating for Kim because of the very slow Wi-Fi and the fact that many places were fully booked, and for me because she insisted on telling me about rubbish Wi-Fi and the fully booked hotels every five minutes or so. Eventually, she found somewhere, and I was glad to hear we wouldn't be sleeping under a hedge. Kim is nothing if not determined when undertaking such tasks and always gets there in the end.

Dinner was in the hotel restaurant, where the friendly waitress explained about the local cuisine and specialities and helped us with our Spanish. It turned out we were now in Basque Country where the locals speak Basque, so no wonder we needed help.

We'd now covered around 2,700 kilometres (1,700 miles), which is further than John O'Groats to Land's End *and back again*, or almost as far as London to Kiev.

The Pyrenees on the road to Pamplona

Day 15, 21 May

Route: Maeztu — Vitoria-Gasteiz — Bilbao — Santander — Comillas
Distance today: 248 kilometres (154 miles)
Distance so far: 2,934 kilometres (1,823 miles)
Bike time: 4 hours 30 minutes
Overnight: La Solana Montañesa, Comillas

Today our destination was to be Comillas on Spain's northern Atlantic coast. To reach Comillas, we would head north-west from Maeztu, join the coast at Bilbao and then more or less follow the coast westwards — a total journey of around 250 kilometres (155 miles). We would have liked to have travelled a little further along the coast, but Kim had had a lot of difficulty finding a hotel which met her rather exacting standards. This was, however, one of those apparently unsatisfactory situations which later turn out to be much better than expected.

I went downstairs for coffee and a smoke at around eight o'clock to find that locals were already congregating in the bar, chatting away and reading the newspapers. One guy already had a schooner of sherry on his table. Maybe this was his weekend treat, or maybe he just liked to get a good start to the day. We decided against sherry for breakfast but tucked into another rustic spread including fruit, cheese, ham, jam, marmalade, toast, home-made cake, fruit juice and, of course, good Spanish coffee. The portions they served us were far too much to eat and, as an added bonus, were included in the room rate. Large hotel operators, please take note.

We didn't have a long ride that day, so we took our time over breakfast and didn't hit the road until ten o'clock. It was a sunny day, although a little windy, but not uncomfortably so, and warm enough for only two layers of clothing which made a pleasant change. As we headed through scenic farmland to Vitoria-Gasteiz along a rural A-road, the wind settled down, so things were looking good.

As we approached Vitoria-Gasteiz, I was looking for road signs to Bilbao, but despite Bilbao being a pretty large and important city, no one had bothered to erect any signs to indicate its whereabouts. I stopped to programme Bilbao into Satnav Woman, and she soon directed us into the centre of town. I was following her directions when Kim tapped me on the shoulder and pointed to a sign directing us to take the next right turn for Bilbao. Satnav Woman, however, was telling me to go straight ahead, so what was I supposed to do? Foolishly, I followed Satnav Woman's advice, and, for the next several minutes, heard Kim providing additional advice behind me. I couldn't hear exactly what she was saying, but I hazarded a guess that it included things like "never listen to me", "always think you know best" and probably much worse than that.

Now that I had road signs, Satnav Woman and Kim all directing me, we soon came out of town and entered a dual carriageway leading us to the AP-68 motorway, which would take us to Bilbao. This route was essentially a 45-kilometre (28-mile) winding descent from the high, country round Vitoria-Gasteiz to the coast at Bilbao. The three-lane motorway was overlooked by tree-clad mountains and was the twistiest motorway I've ever travelled on. I suppose the terrain meant it had to be like this, but it contained some very tight bends of a type not normally seen on motorways, with some speed limits set at 50 and 60 kph (30 and 40 mph). There was next to no traffic, so I kept the speed to a relaxed level and enjoyed the view.

I had to stop enjoying the view as we approached Bilbao because the traffic had become very heavy. We had to leave "our" motorway and join the A-8 towards Santander, which proved to be a rather hairy experience due to the weirdly constructed intersection. Firstly, we merged onto an interconnecting road connecting the two routes from the left (remember that we were in Spain, so entries and exits to and from motorways would normally be on the right-hand side of the road). Secondly, after merging on the left, I immediately saw that the exit to Santander was a very short distance ahead on the right, so I had to scoot across three lanes of busy traffic to take it. Thirdly, and as if we'd not already had enough, the exit immediately took us onto an elevated, single-lane, tightly curving, elevated carriageway. Picture riding a motorcycle along the highest section of a rollercoaster, and you'll get the idea. I imagine that the concrete walls which bordered this funfair ride would prevent car drivers from seeing the long drop to either side, but my added height on the bike meant I had a lovely view over the wall to the river far, far below. Unfortunately, I've never had much of a head for heights.

The traffic was still heavy as we headed out of Bilbao towards Santander, and we soon saw the Atlantic for the first time since we were at Tarifa on Spain's southern coast many days ago. The terrain continued to be extremely hilly, bordering on mountainous, and the road took us through five or six tunnels bored through the towering hills and then along tall viaducts that spanned the deep valleys in between the hills. I've worked on some fairly major construction projects in my time, and consequently, not much impresses me these days, but I had to admit this road was a tremendous feat of both engineering and construction. The road didn't seem to be that old, so whatever the route was before the new road was built must have been tortuous through this hilly environment.

We pulled off the motorway for gas and coffee at about midday and then continued westwards towards our destination. The motorway was still fairly busy, but there were hardly any trucks in evidence — always a good thing as far as I'm concerned. Realising this was the main route to North-West Spain, I imagined that, during the week, the number of trucks would multiply significantly, so I was glad we were doing this part of the journey at the weekend. We exited the motorway at the appropriate place, and about 8 kilometres (5 miles) of country roads took us into Comillas where Satnav Woman behaved perfectly and guided us, without changing her mind once, to La Solana Montañesa hotel where Kim had booked us in for a two-night stay.

Whilst Kim checked us in, I had a stroll round to explore our accommodation. The Solana Montañesa had around ten rooms in a modernish block attached to a traditional old building which formed the lobby, lounge and dining room. The entrance was reached through a roofed, terrace area containing comfortable couches. It provided a spectacular view into the pretty town below and, in the distance, to an imposing building set on top of another hill. An old lady sitting on the terrace saw the direction of my gaze and, pointing to where I was looking, told me that the grand-looking building was a university. She continued to tell me that she and her husband had opened the hotel many years previously. Her husband had passed away several years ago, but the hotel was now managed by her son and daughter; and various other members of the family, including the receptionist, who was her granddaughter, also worked there. I guess she was in her mid-seventies, and judging by the walking sticks by her side, she was probably a little infirm, but she was a sharp as a tack and had a twinkle in her eyes as we spoke. I thought it must be a wonderful feeling for her to be surrounded by a loving family and to still be able to be a part of the business she and her husband had created many years ago. I love being able to have conversations such as this with random Spanish people. People who come to Spain and refuse to learn Spanish then stay within expat cliques and communities miss so much of this very friendly and culturally rich country. Whilst I'm a long way from being fluent, just to be at a level where I can have this type of conversation makes me glad I made the effort to learn. I also read somewhere that learning a new language helps to slow down the effects of dementia, so that's hopefully another benefit.

After unpacking, we found it was only a five-minute walk into the centre of town. Considering we hadn't wanted to stay here and had been looking for somewhere further to the west, we quickly discovered that Comillas was a delightful place. There were many very attractive old buildings, and we immediately noticed that the architecture was very different here. Construction was mainly from stone adorned with a lot of dark, carved woodwork. It looked more like Austria or Switzerland than the parts of Spain we were used to, but then I suppose that, when we were 900 kilometres (560 miles) away from home, there would be differences in the same way as the granite stonework of Aberdeen is different to the timber-framed, thatched cottages of Southern England.

After we'd strolled round the town centre, examining the local plazas for a while, Kim eventually selected a restaurant, and we sat down for drinks, tapas and to watch the world go by, which is one of our favourite occupations. By three thirty, however, the skies had turned black, and when it started to rain heavily, we were forced to move inside. We watched rivers of water cascading from building roofs and running down the streets for an hour, until, as suddenly as the rain had started, it stopped. Our waitress told us we were in for some heavy weather next day, so maybe it was fortunate it wouldn't be a riding day. With a few drinks and some delicious food inside us, we both began to feel the need for a siesta and made our way back to the hotel through the glistening streets for a relaxing snooze.

Our evening was pretty much a repeat of the afternoon — another stroll round town, mingling with the locals out for the *paseo*, and a good dinner at a friendly restaurant.

Over dinner, Kim asked me how I was enjoying the trip so far. 'I'm loving it,' I replied, 'apart from the fact that, just about for the first time in my life, I'm sometimes not enjoying riding my bike.'

'I've noticed you've often been riding slower than usual, and sometimes you seem a bit nervous. I was wondering what was wrong but didn't want to say anything.'

'That's exactly it. I know I don't usually ride that way. The problem is that I don't know why I'm doing it. Maybe I'm losing my riding mojo?'

Kim continued to rub salt into my wounds. 'Well, I can feel your tension on the bike, and you seem to be quite hesitant when going into corners. Usually, I can feel you totally relaxed when riding, as if the bike and you are one single unit. Recently, though, you're stiff and don't seem to be at one with the bike.'

We talked round it for a while to try to get to the bottom of this strange feeling. Have you ever heard a man admit he's either a bad driver or not much good in the bedroom? No, and I'm no different to any other bloke in this respect, so being told I wasn't performing well (on the bike, that is) wasn't something I liked hearing, even if Kim was right. Thank God she didn't have to say, 'It's OK, darling. Don't worry. This type of thing happens to all men at some time or another. Anyway, you can get pills for it these days.' I did, however, know I'm a good motorcycle rider. I've studied the science, practised hard at developing my skills and been told by both the instructors at the California Superbike School and a couple of police motorcyclists that I can handle a bike and have very good road-riding skills. So, what the hell was wrong with me?

Kim put the thought that had been lying in the back of my mind into words. 'I wondered if the moment on the road to Ronda had affected you.'

'Maybe you're right, but we've done a lot of miles since then, and I've had plenty of time to "get back on the horse" and put that behind me.'

Possibly she was right, and this incident had made me lose trust in the tyre-to-road-surface traction equation, and I was subconsciously half expecting the bike to slide on every corner. Failing to get to the bottom of it, we settled the bill and walked back to the hotel for an early night where I probably had nightmares about crashing my bike ... or maybe erectile dysfunction.

Artistic shot of Roadie

Day 16, 22 May

Route: None
Distance today: None
Distance so far: 2,934 kilometres (1,823 miles)
Bike time: None
Overnight: La Solana Montañesa, Comillas

Despite the fact this was Sunday and supposedly a day of rest, I needed to spend a couple of hours doing emails and some work-related matters that couldn't be put off until after the holiday. Kim said she would organise our next stop whilst I was busy, but first we needed breakfast.

There was a television in the dining room, and over breakfast, I watched a Spanish motoring programme. *Top Gear* it certainly was not. Whereas the *Top Gear* guys would be hurtling round a track, smoking the tyres off a Ferrari, this programme showed Spain's version of Jeremy Clarkson dressed in a suit and demonstrating the luggage-carrying capabilities of a Volkswagen Passat by opening the boot and placing a bag in it. Wow! What a very useful feature! He then reversed the Passat out of its parking space and drove it sedately round town whilst talking to camera. The equivalent of The Stig getting every ounce of a car's performance whilst going for the fastest lap round the *Top Gear* test track was another presenter driving a Japanese SUV steadily along a gravelled farm track, no doubt to demonstrate its off-road capabilities. I imagined the equivalent of *Top Gear*'s continental jaunts in supercars or ridiculously unsuitable vehicles would probably be a trip to the post office in a Seat. I could hardly drag my eyes away to discuss the next day's route with Kim.

Looking at the map, it seemed the only sensible road westward was the motorway which more or less followed the coast. Anything else would mean following a backroad route shaped something like a paperclip, and if we were going to complete all of our planned trip, we really needed to make some distance. We decided to head for somewhere in the Viveiro region, which would be 315 kilometres (196 miles) away, because this which would give us a good chance of making it to both the Furthest Point North and the Furthest Point West (Spain) the day after we'd overnighted in Viveiro. With a plan hatched, we retired to our room; me to do some work, and Kim to look at hotels round Viveiro, or maybe catch up on *EastEnders* on BBC iPlayer.

Business completed, we headed down the hill to explore a little more of Comillas. The weather was cool and cloudy with a strong westerly wind blowing straight off the Atlantic, and it definitely looked like it could rain at any time.

As well as researching hotels or catching up on the goings-on in Albert Square whilst I was busy, Kim-Dot-Com had also done some research and found a couple of places for us to visit in Comillas. Our first port of call was El Capricho or, as it's better known, the Gaudí House. It seemed a little strange that, after seeing such a lot of Gaudí's work in Barcelona just a week ago, we were now visiting one of the few Gaudí buildings outside Catalonia. Quite whether the original owner ever anticipated taking possession of a house that looks like something which Hansel and Gretel would find in the forest is unknown, but that's Gaudí for you, and it was an interesting place to visit and reaffirmed my opinion that Gaudí's thinking was so far out of the architectural box that the box wasn't even in the same room.

Next was the Sobrellano Palace which was built during the late-nineteenth century and which has an interesting background. It was commissioned by Antonio Lopez who, aged just fourteen, left Comillas to seek fame and fortune in the Americas. He obviously did all right for himself because, when he returned, he owned several companies, had assisted the Spanish Navy during the Cuban War and had consequently been awarded the title of Marquis of Comillas by King Alfonso XII. If all this wasn't enough, when he returned to Spain, he decided to big himself up even more to his old neighbours and those teachers who, on careers day, told him he would never amount to much if he didn't pull his socks up. He had the palace built to show he'd not done too badly, thank you very much. Just think of the money he would have saved had Facebook or "I'm a Celebrity, Look at Me" programmes been around in the nineteenth century.

After coffee and cake, our random walk led us onto the clifftops from where we could look down onto the harbour. By now, the wind had increased to 70 kph (45 mph), a gale according to *The Weather Channel*. If you aren't sure just how strong that is, we were finding it hard to walk. Suddenly, the wind whipped Kim's scarf away, which resulted in Kim and a passing teenager giving chase. The teenager was pretty light on his toes and soon caught the scarf and presented it back to Kim with a grin and a *de nada* (no problem), when she thanked him. Another good point about living in Spain is that, in our experience, Spanish teenagers tend to do this type of thing as opposed to the types of things that, after she's been reading the *Daily MailOnline*, Kim tells me that the youth of the UK get up to these days.

The wind continued to take our breath away as we walked down the cliffs to the harbour, took a stroll along the beach where we were sandblasted (Kim would have normally paid a fortune for an exfoliation such as this) and back into town, just in time for lunch. Comillas really is a delightful town. The new buildings co-exist sympathetically with the older ones which, unfortunately, can't be said for the blocks of ugly 1960s and 1970s apartment buildings that surround some of Spain's cities.

Unfortunately, by now I was feeling, as my old gran would have said, "proper poorly". My cold seemed to have made a reappearance, and I was experiencing some double vision. I also had a weird feeling of disorientation, and my sense of balance seemed a little disturbed. This sometimes happens when I get a cold, and I think it's something to do with my sinuses. I began to wonder if the balance and feeling of disorientation could be some form of vertigo brought on by my cold, and if so, could this be something that would affect my biking mojo? I didn't know but, to be on the safe side, I popped into the pharmacy for some sinus tablets where, after much pointing up my nose, I discovered that the Spanish for sinus is *el sino,* or maybe it's actually Spanish for bogey.

We were having lunch in the main plaza where we'd found a sheltered spot to avoid the wind. Unfortunately, the lady sitting nearby wasn't in such a sheltered position, and the wind suddenly whipped up the paper tablecloth and wrapped it round her face with some force. The fact she was eating ice cream at the time was even more unfortunate. Her husband had to peel the table cloth off and make sympathetic noises because she was definitely not amused. Kim, on the other hand, was laughing so hard she had to go to the loo, for fear of having an accident. Despite the fact I had man flu again, I, too, managed to raise a small smile.

Kim decided to leave me with my drink and do some shopping. As I washed a couple of sinus tablets down with my beer, I noticed a couple of guys putter past on a classic Moto Guzzi and a classic BMW. Considering the windy conditions, I thought they were either brave or very foolish to be out riding, but it's always good to see old classics being used rather than stored away.

During our walk up the footpath and the steep steps that formed a short-cut back to the hotel, we came across a lady who was stuck because a large branch had been blown by the strong wind from an adjacent tree and was completely blocking the path. After a bit of effort and some choice Anglo-Saxon words, I managed to remove the branch so that we could all pass, and I exchanged a few words with the lady in Spanish. To my embarrassment, she'd obviously recognised my Anglo-Saxon, and when she replied in English, it was obvious she was a rather refined English lady. Apart from the expat tax exiles we'd seen in Andorra, she was the first British person we'd encountered since Barcelona. Who says that Spain is full of Brits these days? Maybe that's true on the touristy costas, but it's not, by any means, in other areas.

As we continued on our way, our new-found friend explained she and her husband had lived in Comillas for twelve years, that her husband had recently become ill, and she was on her way to visit him at the hospital close to our hotel. When she told us she was having to sell her husband's collection of classic cars, it made me wonder if her husband's prognosis wasn't very good. She was a lovely lady, and we wished her all the best when we went our separate ways. Isn't it strange that sometimes you meet someone, and in a matter of minutes, you feel like you have an affinity with them? This was one of those occasions, and although we'd only spoken for a few brief minutes and we would undoubtedly never see each other again, this lady stayed in my thoughts for a long time, and I continued to hope that things worked out well for her and her husband.

When we reached the hotel, I was still feeling pretty grim with my man flu, so I told Kim that, if we were going to have these winds tomorrow and I wasn't feeling any better, I wouldn't be interested in riding anywhere. I then had the sensible notion that a snooze might help me to recuperate.

When I awoke, I was feeling much better. Possibly the sinus tablets had had an effect, or maybe I'd just been tired. My personal travel agent was looking pleased with herself and announced she'd checked *The Weather Channel* and found that winds would be from the north-east at speeds of 25-40 kph (15-25 mph), which would be a vast improvement on that day. Thank you, Wincey Willis. Given this news, we settled on doing just a short leg the next day so that, if I was still feeling under the weather, it wouldn't be too much for my pneumonia and I to cope with. Kim found us a likely-looking place at Muros de Nalón, a reasonable 175-kilometre (109-mile) ride westwards along the coast.

Later, when we strolled back into town for dinner, we noticed the temperature on the sign outside the pharmacy was reading 12 degrees Celsius (54 Fahrenheit). Not exactly the temperature we would have expected to encounter in Spain in late May.

The Gaudí House at Comillas

20

Day 17, 23 May

Route: Comillas — Muros de Nalón
Distance today: 193 kilometres (120 miles)
Distance so far :3,127 kilometres (1,943 miles)
Bike time: 2 hours
Overnight: Hotel Rural Playa de Aguilar, Muros de Nalón

I had a terrible night and hardly slept a wink. Kim kindly let me sleep in until nine forty-five when she woke me up whilst "quietly" packing our bags. Kim doesn't really do "quietly" very well, and I'll give you an example of how living with this affliction can be annoying. If Kim retires to bed before I do, I take pains to take my shoes off before entering the bedroom, pad quietly barefooted through the bedroom to the bathroom in the dark, where I silently undress and have my last pee of the day against the porcelain so as not to make any splashing noises. I then sneak into bed like a very stealthy thing so I don't disturb her. When I'm the one to go to bed first, however, Kim marches through the bedroom as though she's invading Poland, noisily closes the bathroom door after switching the light on, clatters round in the bathroom doing all those things that women find necessary to do before they can go to bed. She then gets into bed as if she's on trial for the Olympic trampoline team, yanks most of the duvet over to her side and then bounces round for a few minutes until she gets comfortable. By now, I'm usually wide awake and wondering if this sort of thing would be sufficient grounds for reducing a murder charge to manslaughter.

At breakfast, the dining room was quiet, and with no Spanish *Top Gear* on the television to keep me occupied, we chatted with the proprietor and his family. Mom, Dad and two daughters were all hard at work, and Grandmother, who looked to be in her seventies, was sitting in her usual chair on the terrace. Over the last couple of days, I'd had a few chats with her and found that she had a lively mind and a wicked sense of humour. Dad complimented us on the fact that we were trying to speak Spanish and observed that most of their foreign guests just seemed to expect the staff to speak the guest's language.

Today's destination was to be Muros de Nalón, a small coastal town near Aviles. Google Maps told us it was 175 kilometres (109 miles) away, and the journey should take around two hours. On the one hand, this was a good plan because I hadn't been feeling up to the mark the day before, but on the other, if we were going to finish the whole trip, we really should be putting in some big distances now. Would we make the whole trip? I was beginning to think not.

We were on the road at a quarter to eleven, and the route towards the motorway was on an enjoyable A-road, taking us past San Vicente de la Barquera, its castle and an ancient bridge over the estuary. I expected the motorway to be very busy with trucks now the weekend was over, but it was quiet, and the only busy spots we encountered were close to the larger towns along the way. Happily, after yesterday's gales, it was a lovely day — bright and sunny with no wind, but it was cold. When we saw snow-covered mountains in the distance to our left, I realised that the cool temperature was possibly not unseasonal. The mountains were the Picos de Europa which rise more than 2,500 metres (8,200 feet) within a distance of only 25 kilometres (15 miles) from the coast.

The motorway roughly followed the coastline between the sea and the mountains, sometimes giving us views of the sea to our right, and sometimes diving inland for a while to take the most direct route. This was yet another spectacular road, and apart from the temperature, it reminded me very much of when we rode the Pacific Coast Highway between Los Angeles and San Francisco. I was so cold that, after about 60 kilometres (40 miles), I stopped at a café so I could don my waterproof jacket for some extra warmth. Typically, after coffee, I forgot to put on the extra jacket, and not wanting to draw Kim's attention to my stupidity, I shivered until the next stop.

The other good news was that my mojo seemed to have returned. Maybe not one hundred per cent, but it was definitely moving in the right direction. We were making good progress, and I was much more relaxed whilst riding. I wondered if my riding problem did have anything to do with the sinus / balance / vertigo thing after all and the sinus tablets had helped.

We arrived at Muros de Nalón at quarter to one. I missed the turning to the hotel, but when I slowed down to make a U-turn, Kim suggested we continue to the beach, for which she'd seen a signpost, and find somewhere for lunch.

Two kilometres (not very many miles) of winding, downhill road led us to a picturesque cove formed by steep cliffs, and we were in luck because the only building to be seen was a restaurant. We sat on the terrace for lunch and idly watched the few people on the beach. By now the sun had retreated behind the clouds that had gradually made an appearance as the day had worn on. There were a few daring souls on the beach, enduring the cold. Some were even in shorts and T-shirts, which I found rather brave. In fact, one brave (or stupid, depending on your perspective) guy was even swimming! I make these remarks because I was still dressed in full biking gear and was feeling the cold. The twenty-odd years I'd spent living in hot countries had obviously thinned my blood or, as my old gran would have told me, "Tha's proper nesh, lad. Tha needs to put thi' vest on."

When we retraced our route back to the small town, Satnav Woman was having an off day, so we had to stop to ask the way to the hotel. The rural lane along which we were directed didn't seem to be a very likely place to find what Kim had described as quite an upmarket hotel, but we pressed on for around two kilometres (again, not very far in miles), passing farms and smallholdings along the way. Just as I was beginning to worry because I could see the lane was about to change from tarmac to gravel, Kim tapped me on the shoulder and pointed to the Hotel Rural Playa de Aguilar on our right. The hotel was quite small, more like another guesthouse really, but appeared to be newly built and very stylish. The location, which afforded a glimpse of the ocean between a tall stand of trees, was secluded. I imagined it would be a great place to come to chill out for a while.

We were greeted by a Michael McIntyre look-a-like who introduced himself as Rogelio, the owner of the hotel. He was very interested in both our trip and the Harley and asked me if I would like to put the bike in the garage of his house next door. Looking to where he was pointing, I noticed an attractive house which was in keeping with the hotel and looked like it had been built at the same time. Rogelio's English was excellent, and our conversation was another one of those where we're doing our best to speak in Spanish and the Spanish person speaks back to us in English. Maybe Rogelio thought our Spanish was so bad that conversing in English was the best option.

Over complimentary drinks, Rogelio explained he used to be a builder, and his job meant he had to spend a lot of time away from home and long hours on the road. When his son was born, he decided to get out of the rat race and do something different. He'd utilised his building talents on the hotel, which had been open for just two years, and also on his house next door. My builder's eye told me that the hotel was very well designed and expensively appointed, and I complimented him on a job well done. It must have cost a fortune, and at only €80 per night and in an isolated location where I doubt people would be queuing up to stay, I hoped he was getting a return on his investment because we appeared to be the only guests. We continued to chat away, and he gave us a potted tourist's guide of the area, its history and the must-see places until it was time for him to leave to collect his son from school.

Rogelio looked to be in his mid-forties, and I had to admire him for deciding to change his life to be able to spend more time *doing* the important things in life rather than working his ass off to be able to afford to *own* the things we think will provide us with happiness. This thought put me in mind of occasions where changes in lifestyle had caused big changes in my own life. One resulted in us moving to Dubai, and another in us leaving. The first was when I was head-hunted and offered a job in Dubai at a significant increase in salary. I soon found, however, that the extra money didn't compensate me for working sixty-hour weeks in a new role that I didn't enjoy. The second was when I realised, after a couple of years of doing it, that I didn't have to work like this, so I handed in my notice and became self-employed, doing the type of work that I did enjoy. The third was when I realised that, owing to the nature of this work, I could do most of it from Spain with visits to the Middle East as opposed to full-time residence. It took me some time to work these things out, but I got there in the end.

As Rogelio was leaving, he introduced me to Marie, one of the hotel staff, and explained she would open the garage so I could put the bike away. When Marie accompanied me to the house, I asked if I could borrow a cloth and have some water to wash the bike. I didn't understand her reply, but because she was pointing to a door leading to the interior of the house that I assumed was locked, I worked out she was telling me I wouldn't be able get any get water until Rogelio came back to open the door. *That's not a problem,* I thought. *I can do it later,* and thanking Maria, I returned to the hotel for ... yes, you've guessed correctly, a siesta.

After my snooze, I went downstairs to see if I would be able to get some water to clean the bike. Rogelio rather embarrassingly informed me that Marie had thought I'd asked her to clean it and did I want to check it was OK? I told him I must have made a poor job of explaining I just needed a cloth and some water so that I could do it myself and set off to find Marie to try to explain and to thank her. I caught her just as she was leaving and hopefully managed put the record straight. Just in case you're wondering, she did a splendid job, and Roadie looked spick and span for the first time since Denia.

When I returned to the hotel, Kim said, 'I wouldn't mind seeing a bit more of this place and having a bit of time off from the bike. What d'you think about staying an extra day?'

By now, if we go back to our "clock of Iberia", we were at eleven o'clock, and we still had to continue round the "Iberian clock-face" anti-clockwise to seven o'clock. This meant we had one third of our journey still to complete, and we still had three Furthest Points to visit. We were seventeen days into our three-week time period, so things weren't looking very achievable. I was about to explain this and object to Kim's suggestion but stopped myself. What was the point in doing this trip if we weren't both enjoying the experience? After all, one of the purposes of the trip in the first place had been to explore Spain and Portugal, and you don't get the full experience from the saddle of a bike. If Kim wanted a day off, well, that would be the right thing to do. Additionally, I'd not been happily married for so many years without knowing those three little words — "Yes, My Dear".

'OK, I'll check with Rogelio, and if it's OK with him, I'll book an extra night.'

Extra night booked and Kim happy, we spent a lovely evening at the hotel, firstly, watching the sun go down over dinner and a bottle of local wine and then chatting to Rogelio about Spanish history and culture. Our conversation was carried out in between watching *Terminator* with Alvaro, Rogelio's young son who, like most Spanish children seem to be, was a polite and good-natured kid. Seeing how much father and son enjoyed each other's company, I couldn't help but think that Rogelio's life-changing decision had been a good one.

Sitting back and finishing my last glass, I came over all philosophical. I turned to Kim and said. 'So, what if we don't finish the whole trip? It's been a fantastic experience so far, and I wouldn't have missed it for anything. In the grand scheme of things, what's a couple of Furthest Points, anyway?'

The beach at Muros de Nalón

Day 18, 24 May

Route: None
Distance today: None
Distance so far: 3,127 kilometres (1,943 miles)
Bike time: None
Overnight: Hotel Rural Playa de Aguilar, Muros de Nalón

Over a hearty breakfast at the hotel, we both agreed that our intentions of keeping up our fitness regimes on this holiday had been less than successful. Kim had managed the odd session in hotel gyms and I had, errr, well ... missed many opportunities. We agreed that a bit of exercise that day would be in order and decided to go for a walk. When I saw that Kim was dressed in full exercise gear whereas I'd dressed suitably for the type of walk I was intending — jeans, trainers and lightweight fleece — I suppose I should have guessed that her idea of a walk wasn't going to be the same as mine. Don't get me wrong, I love walking. I walk for miles with Ziggy, our Spanish water dog, and Kim and I have both enjoyed hiking for many years. When I go walking, however, I do like to ensure I'm comfortably dressed for the occasion, have an idea of where I'm going, how I'm going to get back and a reasonable idea of how long it will take. Kim, on the other hand, just goes for a walk.

It soon became obvious from the cracking pace that Kim was setting that her perception of what we'd agreed to do that morning was more of the hike, or possibly even route-march variety of walk. I, on the other hand, was thinking of a gentle stroll with coffee stops and lunch along the way, probably interspersed with bouts of sitting down and people-watching. I quickly began to get the feeling that the day might end up being less than harmonious.

We made our way along the unpaved lane that started outside the hotel, and as the lane turned to a track, we soon found ourselves walking through some deserted woodland as the track wound its way down to the cove we'd visited the day before. It was considerably warmer than the previous day, and our walk along the beach was very enjoyable. Not so enjoyable, however, was the 2-kilometre (1.2-mile) steep climb at the other end of the beach which we'd dispatched in a couple of minutes the previous day on the Harley. By the time we reached the top, I was feeling out of sorts. I was wearing too many layers for the temperature, so I was hot and sweaty. My jeans were too tight for walking comfortably, and I wasn't in the mood for a hike. In my defence, and in case you're thinking I'm just having another whinge, I would normally have enjoyed a walk such as this, and I would have done it without batting an eyelid, but the way I was puffing and panting made me realise I wasn't quite recovered from the dreaded lurgy that had made its reappearance in Comillas.

When Kim spotted a signpost for a footpath that would take us along a 4½-kilometre (3-mile) route along the clifftops to the next village, she was all for it and raring to go. I quickly worked out that, by the time we'd reached the next village, retraced our steps back to Muros de Nalón and then to the hotel, our walk would end up being around 14 kilometres (9 miles). OK, hardly a route march, but definitely a reasonable hike as opposed to the gentle stroll to which I thought I'd agreed over breakfast. We eventually reached a compromise and agreed we would take a shorter route to Muros de Nalón and then complete the circle along the lane by which we'd reached the hotel the day before.

The village of Muros de Nalón was very agreeable, with the usual selection of cafés, bars and shops set alongside a couple of tranquil plazas. This is a description that could equally be applied to countless other Spanish villages and small towns and is a system that works well. The arrangement encourages a feeling of community amongst the population because it provides a focal point for everyone to come together to eat, drink and to shop, so these areas become a place to socialise. The Spanish have also managed to transfer this feeling of community to city areas that consist mainly of apartments, which is something the UK failed to do in the 1950s and 1960s when blocks of flats replaced countless poor-quality homes. Whereas the British planners usually managed to include a pub, newsagent and maybe a betting shop, the Spanish included cafés, bars, restaurants, plazas, play areas, shops and all those things they traditionally enjoyed from low-rise living within their apartment communities and, what's more, it worked. If you go to one of these areas, people are gathered in the same way as if they were in a town or village-centre plaza.

Kim took the opportunity to stock up a few things from the local shops and left me with my coffee. As I idly watched the local people go about their business, often stopping to chat with friends and acquaintances, I couldn't help but contrast this with our former, hectic, rat-race type of life in Dubai and, for the thousandth time, counted my blessings that we were now lucky enough to be able to enjoy such a wonderful lifestyle in this part of the world.

Sometimes, however, this wonderful life is not very tranquil. I heard people shouting at each other in Spanish behind me, and I turned round, expecting to see some sort of trouble kicking off. I needn't have worried. It was just three middle-aged couples having a conversation, and there were smiles all round. The average Spanish conversation consists of everyone talking at once, and because it's hard to hear and to be heard in this type of situation, everyone tends to raise their voice so they can be heard, and the conversation soon seems to become a shouting match, but in a friendly way. How anyone makes sense of anything beats me, but it seems to work for the Spanish. Maybe they've developed directional hearing like bats so they can hone in to the person they're listening to.

This situation becomes exasperating for me in restaurants, bars and cafés. The average Spanish establishment has tiled floors. They also often have tiled walls and other hard surfaces in abundance, and this makes the sound bounce round so that it becomes hard to hear what people are saying. To have a conversation with your neighbour, it becomes necessary to raise your voice. Of course, this makes it harder for other people to hear what they're listening to, so others in turn raise their voices. Can you see where this is going? The upshot of this is that, as an old, half-deaf bloke, I often find it impossible to hear what anyone is saying at all. My mate Stevie Windows has the same problem, and our conversations often go something like this:

Steve: 'Hey, Andy. Who won the F1 Drivers' Championship in 1984?'

Me: 'Eh?'

Steve: 'I said, who won the F1 Drivers' Championship in 1984?'

Me: 'Lauda.'

Steve: 'WHO WON THE F1 DRIVERS' CHAMPIONSHIP IN 1984?'

Me: 'LAUDA!'

Steve: 'WHO WON THE F1 DRIVERS' CHAMPIONSHIP IN 1984, YOU DEAF TWAT?'

Me: 'JEEZ, MATE, YOU'RE GETTING WORSE THAN ME. IT WAS NIKI LAUDA.'

Steve (inaudibly): 'Pillock.'

Me (also inaudibly): 'Deaf git.'

When Kim returned with her shopping, we set off back to the hotel. By now, I was feeling much better and probably would have enjoyed the longer route after all. Nevertheless, we had an enjoyable walk back. As we passed the various farms, smallholdings and houses along the way, we noticed many of them had what looked to be stone-built sheds raised above the ground on tall stone columns. We'd never seen anything like this before and couldn't work out what they were or what purpose these rather strange buildings served. Some were in good condition and looked as though they were well maintained which indicated current use, and some were quite dilapidated and looked as though they hadn't been used for many years.

Rogelio was in attendance when we reached the hotel, and I asked him about these rather odd structures. He explained they're special to the region and are called *oros*. They're used for storing corn and fruit, and each of the stone columns has a horizontal stone slab set near to the top, which is larger than the column itself. This is to prevent vermin from climbing up and getting at the goodies stored inside. He also explained that the doors all face north, and the *oros* are protected buildings and, although they may be taken down and rebuilt, they may not be removed.

The rest of the afternoon was spent chilling in the hotel with me catching up with some work stuff and Kim-Dot-Com trying to find us somewhere to stay close to La Coruña or Ferrol, a route which would take us by way of the Furthest Point North. Kim was once again struggling to find a decent-looking hotel because they all seemed to be in not particularly attractive industrial areas. I refrained from making the point that we just needed a bed for the night, and the location wasn't that important, because Kim likes to get such things right. Also, she'd done a great job so far on this trip because, in its own way, each place we'd stayed had been really enjoyable.

We'd planned to go out on the bike in the evening to visit a neighbouring village which Rogelio had told us was reputed to be one of the most beautiful in Spain. Unfortunately, it started to rain, so, knowing how even the most beautiful places are likely to be less than pretty when viewed from the point of view of a couple of damp bikers, we decided to give it a miss and stay at the hotel for dinner.

Again, we were the only guests, and we spent some time after dinner playing hunt-the-Star-Wars-figure with Alvaro, which he thought was a great game.

Even though we'd disagreed a tad over the type and duration of our walk, Kim and I had had a great day, and it had done us both good to kick back with another day off the bike. The trip was about us both having a good time and not about setting any endurance records, although tomorrow would see us ticking off another Furthest Point.

Day 19, 25 May

Route: Muros de Nalón — Ribadeo — Punta de la Estaca de Bares — Ortiguera — Ferrol — Bastiagueiro
Distance today: 291 kilometres (181 miles)
Distance so far: 3,418 kilometres (2,124 miles)
Bike time: 6 hours 30 minutes
Overnight: Aparthotel Attica21 As Galeras, Bastiagueiro

After calling at Punta de la Estaca de Bares, otherwise known as the Furthest Point North, our final destination for the day was to be Bastiagueiro, which is near to A Coruña. Google Maps informed us the route would be around 270 kilometres (170 miles) and take around three and a half hours. Looking at the "proper" map and the maze of small roads on the peninsula leading to Punta de la Estaca de Bares, which weren't even shown on Google Maps, I took this with a pinch of salt. Still, this would complete another Furthest Point, so it would undoubtedly be a worthwhile day.

We were up and about by eight thirty, and after breakfast, said our goodbyes to Marie and Rogelio who kindly gave us another bottle of wine. I'd assuaged my conscience for mistakenly asking Marie to wash the bike by leaving her a thank-you note in the room, in my best Spanish, accompanied by a €10 note. We were on the road by quarter to ten, and although it was dry, we were clad in our waterproofs because it was looking distinctly cloudy.

The first hour or so was on the A8 motorway which pretty much follows the coast westwards and led us out of the province of Asturias and into Galicia. There was very little traffic, and the views of the ocean to our right and the green, forested hills to our left made this a perfect opportunity to engage the cruise control at a comfortable 120 kph (75 mph) and relax whilst enjoying a chilled-out ride. The motorway eventually left the coast at Ribadeo, from where it headed south-west towards La Coruña, taking the most direct route between the largest of the towns along the north coast and La Coruña and bypassing a fair-sized chunk of the north-west corner of Spain. I guessed this also meant there wouldn't be much going on in the area further west along the coast, which was the direction in which we were headed. That may well have been true, but after leaving the motorway and heading north-west, we found ourselves on yet another picturesque A-road which continued to hug the coast. The road was good, but this area was definitely not as pretty as Asturias. The small towns and villages contained a lot of industrial units and workshops, and the houses weren't as well designed or as well-kept as those we'd previously seen along the coast. Possibly it was the grey skies, but the area seemed to have an air of poverty and depression about it. If you've ever been to an area in the UK where the local industry has declined, you'll get the idea. Maybe something similar had happened here?

After a stop for coffee, where we removed our wets because the sun had decided to make an appearance, we were back on the N-642 until Porto do Barqueiro where we turned onto a small, rural road which took us onto the peninsula containing our third Furthest Point. The narrow, windy road eventually delivered us at the Punta de la Estaca de Bares, which, at 43° 47′ 38″ north, makes it the northernmost point of both Spain and the Iberian Peninsula and, more importantly for us, our Furthest Point North. Just like the Furthest Point South, this landmark also marks the transition between two seas — in this case, the Atlantic Ocean to the west and the Cantabrian Sea to the east. This conjunction of the two seas apparently makes it one of the rainiest places in Europe with more than 2,500 mm (98 inches) per year. Now, I'm around 1,800 mm (6 feet) tall, so imagine me with my arms stuck straight up in the air and you'll get an idea of just how much water that is. Given this rather grim statistic and our luck with the weather so far on this trip, we were obviously blessed not to encounter any rain on this occasion.

As may be imagined, this is quite a bleak and windy place. It consists of a barren approach with scanty vegetation, and there are just a couple of buildings at the end of the peninsula. There's a lighthouse with a few ancillary structures and some abandoned buildings which were once used by the military as a long-range navigation station. One rather interesting story about this place is that, during World War II, a German submarine was sunk off the coast there. To my mind, this a strange way of putting it because I always thought submarines were designed to sink. Anyway, a German officer who survived used to return every year after that to mark the anniversary and requested that, after his death, his ashes be scattered over Estaca de Bares. I couldn't help but think that, after escaping the sinking submarine, swimming to shore and clambering up the steep cliffs, he would have looked up at the sky and said something like, 'Just my bloody luck! It's pissing down!'

After retracing our tracks back onto the A-road which cuts inland towards Ferrol, we found this was yet another good biking road with very little traffic. The area was, however, sparsely populated, so we spent around thirty minutes looking for somewhere for lunch before we found a place at around two thirty. It was here that Kim came out with one of her more profound statements when she announced she'd just realised that, whilst she loves cheese, likes onions and likes crisps, she doesn't like cheese and onion crisps. '*I* like them,' I announced, making a grab for the packet she'd mistakenly bought, thinking they were salt and vinegar.

We were now beginning to see signs for La Coruña and Ferrol which were historically important places when Napoleon controlled the majority of Europe and Great Britain stood alone in defiance of his all-conquering armies.

The Bay of Biscay was the focal point of the struggle for naval supremacy during the wars of the French Revolution and Napoleon's Empire, and it was here that the Royal Navy had to ensure that the French Navy based on this coast couldn't interfere with the vital approaches to the English Channel. During this period, Spain alternated between being an ally and being an enemy of Britain and, to add to the confusion, during some periods remained neutral. The area of La Coruña where we were heading was the landfall that sailing ships crossing the bay from England would try to make, because it was at this point that they would turn southwards towards the Mediterranean, Africa and, in fact, anywhere in the eastern part of the world. The ports of Ferrol and La Coruña, with their good harbours, needed to be blockaded during the times that Spain was allied with Napoleon to prevent the Spanish and French from impeding England's supply routes. Having ridden through the difficult terrain that exists throughout the whole north-west area of Spain, I understood at first-hand why using overland supply routes to keep the ports provisioned would be almost impossible, so if the ports were deprived of their sea communications by blockade, they would be unable to function as naval bases, and that's exactly what the Royal Navy ensured.

The sight of these names turned my thoughts to what must be one of the most significant events in European history. I suppose that the people who write a country's history books tend not to dwell on the bad stuff, so whilst the name Trafalgar is well established in British history, somewhat unsurprisingly, it's not very well recognised in Spain. Cape Trafalgar is another isolated peninsula between Cádiz and Tarifa, and it was off the coast here that, in 1805, twenty-seven British ships of the line led by Admiral Lord Nelson aboard HMS

Victory defeated thirty-three French and Spanish ships under the French Admiral Villeneuve. The Franco-Spanish fleet lost twenty-two ships, without a single British vessel being lost. Trafalgar was the most decisive naval battle of the war, and the victory not only spectacularly established British naval supremacy but also ultimately denied Napoleon the opportunity of invading and subjugating Britain, as he had done to just about every other European country from the Baltics to Italy. Nelson later died from wounds sustained during the battle, but Nelson's column in Trafalgar Square still commemorates his heroism.

As an aficionado of British naval and military history of this period, to my shame, I was always under the impression that the Battle of Trafalgar was fought in the Atlantic, somewhere off the west coast of Portugal. It wasn't until I was researching for this book that I discovered that Cape Trafalgar, which gave name to the battle which took place 34 kilometres (21 miles) offshore, is actually on the Spanish coast between Cádiz and Tarifa. I've travelled past it several times without knowing the existence of this historic place. In fact, we'd passed very close to it on Day 1 of this trip, and I've therefore promised myself to make a pilgrimage soon to see if there's anything there to mark such a historic event that could have resulted in Europe being a very different place today.

Back on the road, we were heading along the AC-862. This was an enjoyable road for riding, but I couldn't help feeling the place itself was bleak, or maybe it was just the increasingly greying skies that made it seem that way. The gloomy sky had persuaded us to re-don our waterproofs at our last coffee stop which turned out to be a good decision, because, with only 60 kilometres (37 miles) to go to our hotel, it started to rain, and the rain soon turned into a downpour.

Satnav Woman guided us to the AP-9 motorway near to Ferrol and then along seemingly endless roads towards our hotel at Bastiagueiro, just short of La Coruña. By now, I was pretty wet and miserable, and it seemed as though the hotel would never appear. Satnav Woman and my misted-up glasses confused me at a junction, and I mistakenly turned right instead of left at a traffic island, so we were now about to head in the wrong direction. I decided not to filter onto the road and, instead, stopped and put my left indicator on and waited for a gap in the traffic so that I could cross to the other side of the road we were joining. It was then that we encountered the second dickhead of our trip. The guy behind, who could quite easily have passed us on our right to take the filter, decided it would be a good idea to start sounding his horn in protest at my possibly illegal, but certainly not dangerous, manoeuvre. I waved an apology, but this just resulted in more beeping. By this point, I was tired, cold, wet and, consequently, wasn't in the best of moods, so when Kim leaned forward to tell me that he was videoing us with his phone, this was the last straw. I switched off the bike, leaned her over onto the kickstand, dismounted and strode towards the guy in his car with less than charitable thoughts in my mind. I must have looked as threatening as I was feeling because the dickhead suddenly stopped videoing and decided he could pass the bike after all and made a hasty exit. Still, I guess that encountering only two dickheads in eighteen days of travelling wasn't a bad statistic and definitely one that endorses my view that Spain is a very agreeable place and so are the vast majority of its people.

We eventually reached Aparthotel Attica21 at four fifteen. The hotel was located in what looked like an affluent suburb of Galeras, containing some expensive and newish-looking properties. The hotel was modern and well kept, but after the type of accommodation we'd become used to on our journey, it seemed soulless and impersonal. It came with underground parking, which meant I could stay dry whilst unpacking the bike, and we were allocated a good room with a kitchen and sitting area —— not bad at all for only €42 per night.

The area we'd travelled through round Ferrol and La Coruña had been quite industrial and didn't have much to recommend it. This bore out most of the information Kim had gleaned from TripAdvisor that some of the hotels looked OK, but their locations weren't so good because they were situated overlooking workshops or industrial areas. We'd passed some of these en route and wouldn't have wanted to stay. Maybe, as Bill Bryson would say, this is one of those out-on-a-limb places where "no one arrives by accident, and no one goes on purpose".

After unpacking, Kim wisely decided it would be a good idea for me to have a snooze to try to improve my disposition. The rain had stopped shortly after we'd finished riding, which was quite a normal situation on this trip, so Kim took herself off for a walk and to explore the surroundings. I awoke when she returned laden with goodies for dinner that she'd purchased just down the road at a hypermarket. After almost three weeks on the road, I'd run out of clean undies, and my rugby shirt, which was about the only warm shirt I'd brought with me, was looking decidedly grubby. Not being a supporter of the old biker's maxim of making underpants last four days by wearing them the right way round one day, the wrong way round the next day, the right way round and inside out the third day and inside out and backwards on the last day, I decided to pop along to the hypermarket to buy some clean laundry. By the time I returned to the hotel, the fickle weather had changed and had resulted in a lovely, still, sunny evening. I took the opportunity to enjoy this unexpected change and had a couple of small, draught beers whilst sitting in the sun outside the hotel bar. Dinner was hypermarket salad in our room, washed down with the bottle of wine that Rogelio had given us.

Over dinner, we discussed our plans for the rest of the trip. The Furthest Point North that we'd visited that day was at the eleven o'clock position on our Iberian clock, so we still had four "hours" to go to reach home in the seven o'clock position. Unfortunately, however, we only had three days left of our three-week timeframe. If we took the most direct route home from there and stuck to the motorways, we could comfortably cover the 982 kilometres (610 miles) home and stick to our time limit. If, on the other hand, we were going to visit the two remaining Furthest Points, it would mean we would have to travel an indirect and much longer route with fewer motorways, so it had now become impossible to keep within our allotted time and still complete the whole of our intended route.

We'd now been on the road and living out of our bike luggage for eighteen days and were becoming a bit weary of packing and unpacking at a different destination almost every night. Heading for home was an attractive option. It would have been an achievement to have visited the remaining two Furthest Points, but in some respects, the whole Furthest Point thing was a slightly pointless (excuse the pun) exercise anyway, so we discussed the option of heading straight for home in the morning. At this point it was Kim who quoted another of my old gran's favourite sayings — "If a job's worth doing, it's worth doing reyt." Both Kim and my old gran were right! We hadn't come all this way to fall in the final furlong. *Never mind how long it takes! Let's finish the trip and enjoy the rest of the journey. After all, there's not much chance we'll ever do this again, so we might as well do it "reyt".*

Having now made our decision to continue, the next day would see us visiting the Furthest Point West (Spain). Looking at the map after dinner, the route seemed to be through a maze of white- and yellow-coloured roads. There was a motorway for part of the way, but the map marked this as being "under construction". I decided that Satnav Woman, who'd been updated by Satnav Command just before we commenced our trip, would know whether the motorway was operational or not, and we would trust to her good judgement. As I was checking the route, Kim was trying to find the next night's accommodation. The area of our intended overnight destination didn't seem to be very touristy, so she was having difficulty. Eventually, she decided on a self-catering apartment on the coast at Poio, around 60 kilometres (40 miles) north of the Portuguese border.

Punta de la Estaca de Bares, the Furthest Point North

23

Day 20, 26 May

Route: Bastiagueiro — La Coruña — Cabo Touriñán — Santiago de Compostela — Poio
Distance today: 269 kilometres (167 miles)
Distance so far: 3,687 kilometres (2,291 miles)
Bike time: 7 hours 15 minutes
Overnight: Casa O Muino, Poio

It was Kim's birthday and, remembering to remember, I got up first and made coffee so she could have hers in bed. Unfortunately, that was the sum total of her birthday celebrations. I hadn't had the chance to do anything special — yet.

After packing and a lazy buffet breakfast at the hotel, we were on the road and heading out to complete the remainder of our newly revived odyssey at a quarter past ten. Satnav Woman successfully guided us through the busy roads of La Coruña and then, for some reason best known to herself, into a commercial area. Kim, having spotted an IKEA, leaned forward to ask if she could pop in to get some candles, but I feigned deafness and continued to try to find the exit back onto the main road. Having successfully escaped the commercial area, Satnav Woman regained her senses and, after instructing me to "make a U-turn when safe to do so", guided us along a road heading in a westerly direction out of La Coruña and, eventually, into the countryside. We were riding on another great A-road through attractive rural towns and villages. The weather was bright and sunny with only a few scattered clouds. A good road, good surroundings and good weather. What more could a biker ask for? IKEA candles maybe?

Well, a gas station would have been be a good thing because we only had about 20-kilometres (12-miles) worth of fuel left in the tank, and in rural areas in Spain, gas stations are often few and far between. We found one in Vimianzo, however, where we also topped up our caffeine levels at a roadside café. It afforded a splendid view of a castle which, as is befitting a building of such magnificence, had a really posh stone *oro* such as the ones that we'd first seen in Comillas.

As we remounted, Satnav Woman advised us we only had 32 kilometres (20 miles) to ride to reach Cabo Touriñán, which is the Furthest Point West (Spain). The next 10 kilometres (6 miles) were on the A-road, but the next ten were along a maze of small country roads shown as white on our map and which Monsieur Michelin denotes as "other roads". The final ten were on single-track roads as rough as cobbled streets for which an adventure bike with soft, long-travel suspension would have been more suitable. The land was divided into small farms, and we saw the occasional person working in the fields, and they all seemed to be quite elderly – maybe the younger generation have adopted a different way of life. Kim waved as they looked up when they heard the sound of the Harley, and they smiled and waved their greetings to the two strangers on the large, shiny motorbike, possibly wondering what had brought us to this remote place.

It was beautiful, sunny weather at Cabo Touriñán, and we dismounted, removed our helmets and riding jackets and took a stroll round this Furthest Point. There was the obligatory lighthouse but, apart from the tall cliffs, crashing waves and wind-beaten moorland, nothing else marked this important landmark. I guess the alternative would be tacky souvenir shops and mooching tourists similar to Land's End, so although I could have done with a coffee and something to eat, I was happy this remains a place you have to make an effort to visit.

We were now standing on a spot which was almost further west than the west coast of Ireland and, if we were to set off due west from there, our next landfall would be slightly north of New York, some 5,200 kilometres (3,200 miles) away. As I sat on a rock in the sun and pondered these rather impressive facts, Kim disappeared down a rough path towards the sea. I was just beginning to get worried about the length of time she'd been gone when her face appeared over the cliff edge, wearing a huge grin.

'I put a stone on a rock pile someone started down near the water's edge. What a lovely thing to do on my birthday.'

'I'm glad about that,' I replied, 'because I haven't done anything about a present.'

'That's OK, honey. I'm having a wonderful birthday, present or not.'

Actually, I *had* done something about a present, but it wouldn't happen for a couple of days, and I was keeping quiet about it for now.

After enjoying our time at this particular Furthest Point, at which we were the only visitors, we mounted up, and I instructed Satnav Woman to take us to Poio, which was to be that night's destination. A few kilometres along the road, we were obliged to stop to avoid disturbing a rather strange procession. A solitary cow was in the lead, followed by about half a dozen goats, a couple of sheep, and there may have even been a few chickens in amongst the mix. A couple of moth-eared dogs attempted to keep order, and an old boy followed the pack in a beaten-up, old hatchback. I've no idea whether he was taking them out for a walk or whether he had a more productive intention in mind, but we watched them amble along and had to smile until the motley crew turned into a farm track and the road became clear again.

After the country lanes, we were back on what seemed like a fast

A-road with hardly any traffic, although it could have been a B-road because it was yellow on the map. We were heading south-east and eventually reached the motorway approaching Santiago de Compostela. Satnav Woman guided us through a complicated system of off-ramps and on-ramps between several motorways and major roads including a U-turn at a roundabout, all of which sent me dizzy, but she eventually led us onto the AP-9 motorway towards Pontevedra near where our overnight stop was located. This route was so complicated, I couldn't even envisage finding our way without Satnav Woman, so whilst she is often annoying, she does come in handy sometimes.

Had time not been against us at this stage of our trip, I would have liked to have stopped at Santiago de Compostela because, as well as it being a beautiful and historic city, it's also famous for being the destination for pilgrims who have, for hundreds of years, walked the 780-kilometre (480-mile) route of the *Camino de Santiago* (the Way of St. James), which starts at Saint-Jean-Pied-de-Port on the French side of the Pyrenees. Actually, it's supposed to start at the home of the pilgrim in question but there are several other recognised starting points. During our travels through Navarra, the Basque Country, Cantabria, Asturias and Galicia, we'd crossed the *camino* several times and seen several hikers and mountain bikers with scallop shells attached to their packs as a sign that they were undertaking the pilgrimage.

The origins of the pilgrimage stem from the fact that the remains of San Iago (Saint James) are said to be buried in the Cathedral de Santiago de Compostela. Tradition has it that either (a) the remains were brought by boat from Jerusalem after he was beheaded, although why anyone decided that Saint James wanted to be buried in Northern Spain is anyone's guess, or (b) a hermit found some old bones and for some unknown reason they were identified as belonging to Saint James (maybe the clue was in the detached head). Whatever the reason, devotees started making the pilgrimage from the time of the discovery of the remains in 812 AD, and soon, hospitals, hostels and churches sprang up to cater for the needs of the pilgrims. Spain still has a tradition of throwing up hotels and attracting tourists, so maybe this is where it all started.

Pilgrimages continued until the 16th century when the Black Death, the Protestant Reformation and political unrest unsurprisingly led to their decline. As if walking 780 kilometres (480 miles) without a decent pair of Gore-Tex boots or a Swiss Army knife wasn't enough, the early pilgrims were regarded as easy targets for various robbers and bandits along the way and were also subject to epidemics, plagues, pestilence and various other nasty things that were popular in the Middle Ages. Many pilgrims never reached their designation at all. Many arrived at Santiago de Compostela in just the clothes they stood up in and without even the money to buy a bus ticket home.

Happily, the route of the *camino* remained and, in 1987, it was declared the first European Cultural Route and also named as one of UNESCO's World Heritage Sites. Since the 1980s, it's attracted a growing number of modern-day walkers, with over 200,000 people recorded as walking at least part of the *camino* per year in recent times. Facilities such as guesthouses, hostels, campsites, groceries, restaurants and cafés serve the needs of the modern-day walker, and I believe that bandits and brigands are no longer permitted to ply their trade. Whether modern-day walkers still do this as a pilgrimage, a challenge, or just because they fancy a decent walk, I don't know, but anyone who completes the full *camino* certainly deserves respect.

The route ends at the Cathedral de Santiago de Compostela, where mass is held twice a day for the faithful. During the mass, a huge incense burner, which needs four people to swing it on its long rope, fills the cathedral with its heady aroma. Whilst this may sound like a quaint tradition, its origin stems from the fact that, in years gone by, the pilgrims smelled so bad after their journey that incense was needed to mask their ripe body odour. Another tradition was that some pilgrims would undertake a further three-day hike to Cape Finisterre and throw their stinking clothes into the sea. It's not recorded how they avoided getting arrested on public indecency charges. Possibly an enterprising Asian family opened a shop selling cheap clothes so that they could re-outfit themselves?

We stopped for lunch along the AP-9, looking forward to an easy 100-kilometre (62-mile) stretch to Poio. So far it had been a great biking day, and it was good to be continuing out intended itinerary rather than just making miles towards home. As I sat, I felt something moving between the wide stem of my sunglasses and my head. When I removed my sunglasses, a stunned bee fell out. We'd ridden through another swarm, and I was thankful this one hadn't exacted his revenge on my head.

As we set off again, the wind got up, and clouds started to darken the sky. I hoped *The Weather Channel* had been right about it remaining dry. It did stay dry, but the last leg of our journey was spent battling high winds again, which spoiled an otherwise perfect day's riding.

Another thing that spoiled a perfect day's riding was that, when we reached Poio, Satnav Woman guided us up and down some very narrow village roads. When she finally announced, 'You have reached your destination,' we couldn't see anything that looked remotely like a guesthouse. We parked the bike and walked up and down lanes looking for Rua O Muino, which was the road on which the guesthouse, Casa O Muino, was supposedly located, but found absolutely nothing. I was forced to execute a very tricky three-point turn on a narrow, steeply sloping road, which isn't something to be recommended on a heavy touring bike loaded with luggage. As a bike has no reverse gear, and it's impossible to paddle a heavy bike backwards and uphill, it's necessary to make sure that all the uphill parts of the turn are done in a forward direction, allowing the bike to reverse by gravity. I was hot and sweating in my bike gear and not in the best of moods after managing to get the bike pointed in the right direction.

My mood hadn't improved much when, an hour later, we had still not located the guesthouse. Further consultations with Satnav Woman kept directing us back to the same place where she continued to insist we'd reached our destination. I eventually flagged down a passing motorist and asked if he could direct us to Casa O Muino.

'*Sí, sígueme,*' he replied with a smile. Guessing that this meant "follow me", I mounted up, started Roadie, and he led us along a circuitous route before stopping on the main road into town, where he pointed at a house bearing a sign saying, "Casa O Muino". At this, our saviour waved and went along his way with our heartfelt thanks following him down the road.

The guesthouse wasn't exactly a guesthouse as such but a large house that had been divided up into small, self-contained, self-catering apartments, and the owner was waiting to show us round and give us the key. We apologised for being late and explained the reason. The owner told us that satnavs don't have the correct street address, which is Rua O Muino and, instead, direct all the guests to Barrio de Muino, which is the nearest match. 'Then why the **** don't you tell your guests about this on your bloody website?' I felt like saying but didn't.

The apartment was fine, however, and we soon got settled in. I asked the owner what the very large, old building was that we could see from the window. He explained it was a monastery. *Bloody hell,* I thought. Being a monk must have been a very popular occupation at one time because the building was huge. I wondered just how many brothers lived there in these more modern times.

Once we'd settled in, Kim left me to check my emails and walked into town for a look round. She returned an hour or so later with dinner consisting of cheese, crisps, French bread and a bottle of red wine. We settled down to eat and watched the BBC on iPlayer before having an early night. It wasn't much of a birthday celebration, but Kim did get to visit the Furthest Point West (Spain) and put a rock on a pile of other rocks, and she likes doing things like that.

Cabo Touriñán, the Furthest Point West (Spain)

24

Day 21, 27 May

Route: Poio — Pontevedra — Porto — Aveiro
Distance today: 258 kilometres (160 miles)
Distance so far: 3,945 kilometres (2,451 miles)
Bike time: 3 hours 45 minutes
Overnight: Hotel das Salinas, Aveiro

Our destination today would be Aveiro, and our route would take us back into Portugal for the first time in more than twenty days. Google Maps advised us it would be a journey of 242 kilometres (150 miles) and the route would be mainly on motorways, so it wouldn't be a long day in the saddle.

We were up early at eight thirty and, looking outside, I could see it was bright and sunny with no wind. It was also quite chilly, but it looked as if it would be a good day for riding.

There was coffee in the apartment, but we didn't have anything to eat, so our first destination was a café in the town for breakfast. Kim ordered coffee and toasties for each of us, but what came was coffee, orange juice, toasties, croissants, butter and jam. When Kim asked if she could have tomato on her toastie, the lady proprietor nipped across the road to the grocery store to buy some. A fantastic breakfast with excellent and friendly service and all for the princely sum of €5 for both of us. This sort of thing tends to be the norm rather than the exception in Spain. Unfortunately, I couldn't do the breakfast the justice it deserved. It was just too much for me. I'd lost my appetite, probably due to lack of exercise and eating too much unhealthy, convenience food for the past three weeks.

We were on the road properly by ten thirty, and Satnav Woman took us on a diverse route through Poio, round Pontevedra's bay and over its river. Judging by the small roads she was directing us along, I was sure there must have been a quicker route, but both Poio and Pontevedra are very pretty, and as we didn't have a long ride ahead, I just relaxed and enjoyed the experience and the sights.

When we reached the AP-9 motorway, which was the same one we'd arrived on, we were heading due south through tree-covered hills. It was still very green in this area and more reminiscent of Northern Spain than the south, which at that time of year, tends to have become parched and brown. The motorway was very twisty due to the hilly terrain and took us over many vertigo-inducing viaducts.

We crossed the border into Portugal and stopped for gas and coffee at eleven forty-five, about halfway to our destination. As I was gassing up, I thought to myself that I should have filled up before leaving Spain, where fuel is cheaper. I haven't lived in Yorkshire for over twenty-five years, but I just can't lose the Yorkshireman's ingrained hatred of paying more than necessary for anything. When I went to pay, however, I realised that things had evened themselves out a little, because the gas station sold cigarettes and not only are these cheaper in Portugal, but they're also easier to come by. In Spain, you can only buy tobacco from tobacconists and vending machines in gas stations, cafés and bars. If you're an addict, this means that panic sets in if you find yourself running out of cigarettes when everywhere is closed.

As we were leaving the gas station, I noticed the bike was running very fast on tick-over and hoped this wasn't going to become another expensive technical problem. Running all my other Harleys had cost me almost nothing, apart from routine servicing. Roadie, however, which was the latest, brand-new and much-improved model when I bought it, was a different story. My thinking when I bought the bike was that, because it was my intention this would probably be the bike I would keep until I retired from biking, I might as well get the newest model with all the upgrades and improvements that came with it. It had, however, cost me an arm and a leg over the years due to various problems, even though I'd racked up less than 30,000 kilometres (18,600 miles).

The original front brake discs warped at quite low mileage, so I upgraded them to a pair of Harley chrome floating discs. These looked great but also warped at not very many more kilometres later. This wasn't a major expense, but three pairs of brake discs in 25,000 kilometres (15,000 miles) is a bit much. The engine control unit had fried when I'd stupidly jet-washed the bike. That was expensive, but as it was totally my fault; I can't really blame Harley-Davidson.

I'd always planned to take Roadie to wherever our destination was to be when it became time to leave Dubai, so when we decided to move to Spain, I researched the regulations with regard to customs duty for vehicles. My research, backed up by the shipping company's advice, revealed that, so long as I'd owned the vehicle for something like a minimum of twelve months before I imported it and kept it for another twelve months after importation, it would be regarded as a personal possession so, just like the rest of our worldly goods that were being imported, I wouldn't have to pay any duty. Great news then!

It turned out not to be such good news when the shipping agent in Spain called me to say I needed to pay €2,400 before customs would release the bike which was in a container in Seville together with all our other stuff.

'But I've researched this, and because I've owned the motorcycle for more than twelve months, it's a personal possession, and I shouldn't have to pay any duty.'

'Yes, this is the EEC regulation, but the Customs here apply duty anyway, so the only way we can get your container released is if you pay the duty.'

'But this is against European regulations.'

'Yes, I know this, and you can make a case against the Customs authorities if you wish.'

The lady at the shipping agents was most helpful, and I could tell she had sympathy for my situation. She'd probably had this conversation many times before.

Quickly weighing up the chances of bringing a successful case against a government authority in a country where my language skills were very basic, and the time and money it would take to do so, together with the fact that we needed our shipment, there was only one solution.

'How do I pay the duty?' I asked the lady.

I don't want to report this as actual fact, but I was informed later that this is one of several ways that Spain flout EEC regulations. Yes, it's against EEC rules to charge duty in such circumstances, and yes, the Spanish are fined by the EEC for doing so, but as the fines are considerably less than the income they receive from the illicit duty, they happily pay the fines. Apparently, this applies to other EEC regulations that Spain either doesn't agree with, or which don't work in its favour. If this is true, and despite being out of pocket in this instance, given the many stupid rules and regulations that the ECC seem to come up with, I admire a country which says, 'We don't like that, so we're not doing it.'

Once I'd paid the duty, I expected that registering the bike in Spain would be relatively straightforward. Again, I was being naïve. I was obliged to surrender my Dubai number plate when I obtained the export certificate, so I couldn't ride the bike as if I was a tourist in Spain. I also found out that I couldn't insure it without it having a registration number, so I couldn't even ride it to the test centre where it would be inspected and, if all was well, issued with a Spanish registration number.

I obtained the services of Meri, a Spanish guy who's in the motor trade and, because he speaks very good English and German, has a nice little side-line helping expats buy and sell cars, getting them serviced and taking them for their annual ITV, the equivalent of the MOT test. Meri made the appointment for the inspection, told me all the documents I would need to take with me and arranged for a recovery vehicle to transport the bike to the testing station. Off we went, with me fully expecting to come away with a shiny new number plate ready to stick on Roadie so that we could take to the roads of Spain. It was not to be, however.

When I bought Roadie, I'd known it would be more than likely that the bike would end up in Europe, so I'd ordered it with European specification and envisaged no problems when registering it in Spain. By the time we arrived, I'd owned the bike for around four years and, during this time, had tinkered quite a bit. Immediately I took possession, I paid what the Americans call "Harley Tax", which involves changing the standard exhausts to a more free-flowing pair, changing the standard air filter to a less restrictive type and fitting a tuneable engine control unit. These modifications release a few more horsepower over the standard state of tune and also make it sound the way that enthusiasts think a Harley should sound. I'd also changed quite a few standard features for better, or custom, parts. The upshot of all this was that, at the test centre, I was presented with a list of reasons why Roadie couldn't be registered in Spain. To be fair, the inspector also said that the noise level from the exhausts was right on the border of failing and that he realised that the K&N Air Filter was non-standard, but he would let these go. He seemed to be a mate of Meri's, and I think he appreciated my attempts to speak Spanish. As a biker himself, it also looked as though he quite liked Roadie.

Because of business trips, it took me a few weeks to source replacement parts on eBay, fit everything and repeat the inspection process. Happily, this time round, all was well, and I was soon able to fit my Spanish registration on Roadie's rear mudguard, obtain some insurance and hit the road.

Talking of roads, do you remember the road to Ronda? Well, on one occasion, I was in Ronda on my way to Marbella and was looking forward to heading down this very same road when the front brake lever locked up solid. The brakes weren't on, but nor could I operate them. I contemplated pressing on, just using the back brake, but this road is like an alpine pass, and as I was heading downwards, I reasoned that the front brake would probably come in quite handy. I called my insurance company's recovery service who rescued me and took the bike to a Harley workshop in Marbella where they diagnosed the problem as being a faulty ABS unit. There wasn't one available in Spain, so it had to be specially ordered, and it would take some time to arrive. I don't remember the exact cost of the repair, but it wasn't cheap, even without the cost of the two-week car hire which I needed to get home and subsequently return to collect the Harley.

The next problem was on the way back from a HOG rally in Cádiz, when, around 100 kilometres (62 miles) from home, the bike refused to go above 40 kilometres (25 miles) per hour, and we had to limp home using the hard shoulder of the motorway, all the time expecting the bike to die on us at any moment. When I later trailered the bike to the Harley dealership, the diagnosis was that the fuel injection unit had packed up and, guess what? There wasn't a replacement unit in Europe, and once again, it had to be specially ordered. This time the bill was €720, and it took them five weeks to get the part and fix the bike.

This is only my personal opinion, but given the fact I've owned five Harleys, it seems to me the quality has deteriorated over time. My Dyna is fifteen years old now and has done over 60,000 kilometres (37,000 miles), but some of its parts are still in better condition than Roadie's.

This also seems applicable to modern cars. As well as being a long-term motorcycle lover, I'm also a car nut, and I especially like classic and modern-classic cars. I currently own a 1994 Mercedes SL which was made during the era when Mercedes was managed by engineers, rather than accountants, and their vehicles were built with engineering and quality as the prime concern. This was also before the time when electronic and computer wizardry became prevalent in cars. I'm pretty confident that, if my Mercedes is serviced and looked after properly, it will still be on the road for many years to come. My modern BMW, however, will probably eventually be consigned to the scrap heap when some complicated electronic part fails and it becomes uneconomical to repair. Such is progress, I suppose, and don't get me started on the latest systems that allow cars to almost drive themselves, because I never want to own a car that has anything like that.

Back on the road towards Aveiro, Roadie seemed to have cured her reluctance to tick over properly, and we were now travelling through undulating hills rather than steep ones, and there were far less trees in the surrounding countryside. The motorway only became busy round Porto, which is Portugal's second largest city after Lisbon, so this continued to be a good ride. The motorway had straightened out now due to the less difficult terrain, and we were cruising along at 130-40 kilometres (80-90 miles) per hour, and I was totally enjoying the ride.

I suddenly realised this was the first motorway we'd been on which had allowed us to cruise at these speeds for any length of time for about the last two weeks. Since the Costa Brava, all the motorways had been very twisty and not at all what I was used to. They included steep ascents and descents, viaducts with breath-taking and vertigo-inducing heights and stiff crosswinds. Many of the sections through mountains or cities had quite narrow, claustrophobic lanes, and some sections had 80 kilometres (50 miles) per hour speed limits because of various hazards and tight bends. The truth was that, whilst these types of motorways usually afford amazing vistas, they just aren't made to be ridden at the sort of speeds at which we were now comfortably cruising.

To spoil a good day, we ran into some rain just short of Aveiro, but I could see blue skies ahead and noticed the oncoming traffic didn't have their windscreen wipers on, so I hunkered down behind the windscreen and kept going. The rain didn't last long, and my shower-proof jeans and jacket both did their job.

After checking into a fab suite at the hotel, courtesy of an upgrade due to Kim's Genius status on booking.com, we took a stroll round Aveiro.

It's an ancient but small city set on an estuary and whose main purpose used to be to produce salt and harvest seaweed for use as fertiliser. Over time, buildings were constructed alongside its natural waterways, and the waterways were turned into canals, which now form part of the city. It's not exactly Venice in that it's not as pretty and not as historic, but it's very attractive nevertheless and all the better for not being full of tour groups tramping round with totally miserable looks on their faces, (Why is it you never see anyone on one of these guided tours who looks as if they're enjoying the experience?) Some of Aveiro's buildings were obviously very ancient, but many were built in the Art Nouveau and Art Deco styles during a period of prosperity for the city in the late-nineteenth and early-twentieth centuries, and these were particularly attractive. Unlike many cities, more modern buildings have been constructed with sympathy to their surroundings, and the whole mix works harmoniously. Many of the streets and pedestrian areas have modern, urban landscaping, and this also manages to balance with both ancient and modern edifices. This careful planning has produced a very attractive place with a very agreeable feel about it.

After strolling round for a while and soaking up the atmosphere, we selected a restaurant for lunch. I ordered *fruit de mer*, which was both tasty and refreshing. When I remarked that I didn't see how crab sticks qualified as seafood, Kim's response was, 'Well, what do you expect for €5.50?'

'I expect what it says on the menu, and crab sticks are fruits of the factory and not fruits of the sea.'

It was very tasty, nevertheless.

A type of boat which is fairly unique to Aveiro had developed over the years. These are known as *moliceiros* and they were built for use in the shallow waters during salt production and seaweed gathering. They're long and narrow, with a shallow draft and, although not as long, are similar in proportion to British narrow boats. These days, they ferry tourists round rather than salt and seaweed, so we decided to take a tour round the city on one of these brightly decorated craft. We'd just bought our tickets and were waiting by the side of the main canal for our particular boat's departure time when the skies blackened, and the rain suddenly came down in torrents. We dashed to take shelter in front of a shop that had a small overhang above the window and pressed ourselves back against the glass, successfully managing to avoid the worst of the downpour. Not so lucky was the lady standing next to me. She had rather large boobs and, however much she pressed her back into the shop window, she couldn't quite avoid the rain that was coming down like stair rods. To add insult to injury, the wet-T-shirt look was being exacerbated by the water dripping from the overhang above the window. Judging from the effect on the lady's anatomy, I guessed the rain must have been quite cold, too! *Every cloud has a silver lining*, I thought as I studiously tried to avoid staring.

Either fortunately or unfortunately, depending on your point of view and who you were standing next to at the time, the rain didn't last for very long, and we were able to take our places on the boat for the tour. As we boarded, we wished everyone a cheery good afternoon, and although the captain returned our greetings with a big smile, the other two couples, who were the only other passengers, studiously avoided eye contact and remained silent. It soon became apparent they were English, but although it must have soon become obvious that we were also English, neither of them seemed inclined to enter into conversation, so after a couple of attempts to chat to the first English people we'd met since the lady in Comillas six days earlier, we gave up and left them to their own company.

This type of behaviour is something we'd noticed about many English people since we'd moved to Spain. Many years ago, when we lived in the UK, it was fairly normal, especially in the north, for people to say hello and to chat when finding themselves in the company of strangers. From my infrequent visits to the UK recently, it seems as though, if you attempt to speak to a stranger, they think you're some kind of nutcase or worse. In Spain, or at least in our part of Spain, everyone says *hola* as they enter a shop or café or join a queue and, if you're out walking, it's usual to smile and wish other people *buenos días* (good day) as you pass and receive the same in return. If you do this with many English, however, they're likely to completely ignore your presence, or you'll be met with stony silence. Such people can't even use the excuse they don't understand the language, because it's pretty obvious when someone is saying "hello" or wishing you "good morning / afternoon / evening", whatever language is being spoken. It's also the case that the person greeting you will probably understand the sentiment, if not the exact words, if you reply in your own language. Anyway, the fact the Spanish are generally very polite and friendly is just another reason I enjoy Spain.

Pedro, the captain, was a jolly chap and very informative about both Aveiro's history and present-day life there as he guided us up and down the canals and pointed out various beautiful and interesting buildings, the brightly painted timber fisherman's houses, the old ceramics factory with its tall chimney and various other sights and places of interest. Occasionally, passengers on other boats and passers-by, especially children, would wave to us, but our fellow English passengers failed to respond. Kim and I probably over-compensated by waving back as though we'd just spotted some long-lost friends. Apart from the company, the forty-five-minute tour was very enjoyable and excellent value for only €6 each. I bunged Pedro an extra couple of euros as I thanked him upon disembarking. I noticed the other Brits didn't, but that was what I'd come to expect by then.

In the evening, we took another stroll round town and had a few drinks in one of the squares before deciding to treat ourselves to a Chinese dinner. There are a lot of Chinese people in Spain and

Portugal, and as well as Chinese restaurants, every town has a selection of "full-of-crap" shops. Even small communities tend to have Chinese emporiums that sell cheaply priced stuff that will break the first time you attempt to use it. It's perfectly reasonable to expect a Chinese person to speak Spanish or Portuguese with a Chinese accent, in pretty much the same way they do when speaking English. For some strange reason, it's a constant source of amusement to me when someone in one of these shops thanks me by saying "*glacias*" or "*obligado*". Little things I suppose.

The restaurant was much the same as any other Chinese restaurant from the 1980s or '90s, i.e. lots of red and black décor; glossy, black furniture and weird Chinese art hanging crookedly on the walls. The service was good, however, and the food was excellent. I know I promised not to list everything we ate on the trip and how much we paid for each meal, and I know I've mentioned prices a few times already in this chapter, but, come on, €27 for two, two-course meals and a bottle of wine just has to be mentioned. I doubt if you could even get a Chinese takeaway in the UK for that price, much less get a bottle of wine with which to wash it all down.

As I wrote up my notes before going to bed, I worked out we'd so far covered around 3,900 kilometres (2,500 miles), which is the same distance as Sydney to Perth, or Chicago to Los Angeles via Route 66. These rather impressive statistics made me happy we'd decided to carry on with our full itinerary and hadn't cut our journey short.

Aboard the moliceiro in Aveiro

Day 22, 28 May

Route: Aveiro — Sines — Cabo de Roca — Cascais
Distance today: 318 kilometres (198 miles)
Distance so far: 4.263 kilometres (2,649 miles)
Bike time: 5 hours 45 minutes
Overnight: Casa Vela Charm Guesthouse, Cascais

I was up at nine o'clock and then realised it was only eight o'clock because we were now back in Portugal, and I'd forgotten to adjust my watch from Central European Time back to Western European Time.

Kim was in bed and looking at something on the Internet. I assumed she was searching for somewhere to stay, but when she asked me to check something out, I realised she was looking at sofas — apparently, the sales were on. Now we were getting near the end of our trip, she was obviously thinking of new projects for the house.

It was a grey, drizzly and miserable day, and when we passed reception on our way to breakfast, the receptionist informed us that this unseasonal weather was set for the next two days. *Well, it looks as though we'll be finishing the trip in the same way as we began it,* I thought as I headed for breakfast.

An hour or so later, we were packed and ready for the off. I'd retrieved the waterproofs from the bike, and we were in the overly warm hotel reception where I was attempting to put my waterproof over-trousers on. I've previously mentioned the fact that waterproof bike trousers are always too short, but what I didn't mention was the fact that, even with the trouser bottoms unzipped, they're never wide enough to get over size eleven boots. As well as being wet outdoors, it was also quite chilly, so I was wearing three or four layers of clothing including my heavy bike jacket. Consequently, I was sweating away in the sauna-like reception area as I struggled to get my trousers over my boots. I eventually made it, but when I stood up and pulled them up, I realised they were even shorter than usual. I'd put on Kim's by mistake! Now I had to remove them and go through the whole process again. Kim, of course, fell about laughing whilst repeating, 'Gromit! They're the wrong trousers,' which would have been quite funny had I not had sweat running into my eyes and down my back.

After I managed to sort out my trousers, we set off at ten fifteen, and although we were riding in and out of cloud and it was quite chilly, the rain was, thankfully, holding off. After an hour or so, we had to stop for gas and, as usual, took the opportunity to grab a coffee.

Coffees consumed, we were back on the road and found ourselves riding into a strong headwind which, on a bike, always makes it feel as though you're going faster than you are. Satnav Woman directed us off the motorway near Sintra and then along narrow, twisty roads for around 12 kilometres (7½ miles) through the Sintra-Cascais Natural Park until we reached Cabo de Roca, which is — wait for it — drum roll please — the Furthest Point West (Mainland Europe). Yay! Our fifth and final Furthest Point!

Whilst the approach to Cabo de Roca through the national park was fairly typical of the other Furthest Points we'd visited, the actual location was a far cry from the other points. In addition to the obligatory lighthouse, we arrived to see a large, busy car park, souvenir shops, a café, and the whole place was teeming with people. I suppose the proximity to Lisbon makes this a popular destination for people visiting the area, and judging by the number of tour buses parked up, the tour operators obviously thought so, too.

The lighthouse, which is set on the peninsula atop 100-metre (328-feet) high cliffs, is the oldest one in Portugal, and there are also the ruins of a seventeenth-century fortress close by. As is usual with Furthest Points, the area, although quite bleak, is stunningly beautiful, with wide vistas north and south along the coast and out to sea. Due west, at the other side of the Atlantic Ocean, is Washington DC. We were now at the most extreme westerly point of continental Europe, and if it weren't for the fact that Dunmore Head in County Kerry, Ireland, lies just one degree of longitude further west, we would also be further west than the most westerly part of Ireland. Apparently, until the fourteenth century, Cabo de Roca was thought to be the edge of the world. Obviously then, County Kerry hadn't been discovered at that time, which must have been a bit of a disappointment to Saint Patrick and anyone living there.

The weather had brightened up considerably, so maybe the miserable grey stuff the receptionist at the hotel in Aveiro had told me about had only been forecast for the local area. We removed our waterproofs and took a stroll round the various pathways set along the cliff tops. As we wandered round, we noticed that the route of the Caminho do Atlântico passes through the site. I'm not sure if this is another pilgrim route, but it follows the west coast of Portugal, and if the route goes through landscapes such as this, it must be a stunning and challenging walk.

We took some photos to record our final Furthest Point, and I was trying to take a couple of shots of Kim standing against the tall stone marker bearing its name when a Chinese woman in a stupid hat attempted to shoo her away. She obviously thought she had more of a right than Kim to have her photo taken there. I see a lot of Westerners in the Middle East who make no effort to respect local customs and culture, so I suppose this was an example of the fact that tourists from all over the world sometimes just don't consider that their ways may not be acceptable in other places.

After our stroll, photographs, altercations with the rude lady and a quick coffee and a pastry in the tacky café, we mounted up and set off for the day's final destination, which was to be Cascais. We'd never visited Cascais before, but we'd heard a lot about it. It's not only supposed to be very pretty but also home to Portugal's Rich and Famous and, therefore, a place to be and to be seen. The direct route was only around 20 kilometres (12 miles), but we had plenty of time in hand, and the weather had turned warm, and the sun was shining, so I asked Satnav Woman to take us there via the longer, coastal route. This was a good choice because, after descending to sea level, we were riding past rocky bays and beaches with the sparkling Atlantic our constant companion to our right. As we approached Cascais, we began to see Hollywood-style houses, so the Rich and Famous reputation seemed to be well founded.

The Rich and Famous have obviously had a word with the satnav people because Satnav Woman guided us through the town centre, into a leafy suburb and announced, 'You have reached your destination,' right outside the gate of the Casa Vela Charm Guesthouse which reflected its name and was very charming indeed.

The young lady on reception informed us it was a family-owned and run hotel and took us on a tour through the comfortable dining room, the opulent sitting room and other tastefully decorated and furnished public areas. She even showed us three individually decorated rooms and invited us to select the one we preferred — try getting that sort of service in chain hotels. The only available parking was on the road, but seeing we were bikers, she asked me if I would like to park the bike in the grounds, an offer I gladly accepted. The hotel had been created from a large, old house with a very modern extension added on for additional guest accommodation. This combination of old and modern shouldn't have worked, but it did, and the whole place was delightful. Another great selection by Kim-Dot-Com.

After a chillax on the balcony overlooking the pool and gardens, a bit of a snooze and a shower, it was early evening, and we were ready to take a walk into town. Kim knows that Portuguese pavements and squares are almost invariably constructed by a technique known as *calçada* from small limestone and basalt stones, which are similar to cobblestones, so why she decided high heels would be a good idea, I don't know. I did, however, have a sneaky suspicion she didn't want to seem underdressed if the Rich and Famous were in town. She looked very chic and trendy that evening. How she pulled it off from our limited luggage and after three weeks on the road, I have no clue, but the ability to look great in all circumstances has always been one of her many talents.

Owing to said high heels, our walk was more of a stroll, but we managed to have an ice cream at the side of the small beach, a walk (sorry, stroll) past the large marina, explore the area surrounding the castle and admire the many opulent old houses surrounding the town centre. We eventually settled down for an early dinner at a restaurant in one of the squares, where we were handed a basket containing rustic Portuguese bread and tuna pâté. This reinforced the fact that we were back in Portugal because both the bread and the pâté were gorgeous, and it's almost inevitable you'll be offered this when ordering a meal. I opted for pork and clam stew, which is a traditional Portuguese dish and was delicious.

After dinner, Kim suggested another stroll but this time around the town centre. Cascais is very trendy, and I soon discovered Kim's game-plan when we began to pass numerous boutiques. I consequently spent a long time propping up walls and lamp-posts whilst Kim "just popped in for a look". Still, it wasn't a total waste of time, because a classic Triumph puttered by, closely followed by a classic Moto Guzzi, and there were also a number of good-looking modern and classic cars cruising round for me to admire. The Rich and Famous did indeed seem to be in residence that evening.

Not only was this the first upmarket place we'd stayed in since

Barcelona, it was also the first time since Peñíscola, some fifteen days ago, that we'd been in what felt anything like a holiday resort. The holiday atmosphere was reinforced when we happened upon an area containing a selection of bars with names such as "John Bull", "The Duke" and "The Chequers". It seemed this was an attempt to attract British tourists, and it obviously worked because we overheard quite a few British accents. Apart from the miserable people on the boat in Aveiro and the lady in Comillas, we hadn't spoken to any Brits for a very long time, so we decided to play at being holidaymakers and stop for a drink. One of the things that I do miss about the UK is a decent pint of proper beer so, because we were outside the Red Lion, I asked if they had any British beer. Unfortunately, however, this "pub" didn't quite do what it said on the tin, so I had to make do with local Sagres lager, which although I've become accustomed to it, isn't a patch on proper Yorkshire beer with names like Old Sheep Dip. Even this didn't put a damper on the evening because there was a lively atmosphere in the square, and this was a far cry from many of the more tranquil places we'd recently visited. Each pub had at least one television which could be watched from the crowded outside tables, and the couple on the next table told us this was the evening of the European Cup Final between Atlético Madrid and Real Madrid — a real Spanish affair. The Portuguese would be rooting for Real Madrid because their favourite son, Cristiano Ronaldo, would be playing.

As we relaxed with our drinks, we started to play one of our favourite games — Spot the Brit. Kim usually wins because, whilst the British guys are usually dead giveaways, she understands ladies' fashion, or lack of it, much better than I do. We've become uncannily good at this game because British tourists seem to have a knack of looking exactly like, errr, well, British tourists I suppose. For what it's worth, therefore, and based on many years' experience of living outside Britain and travelling extensively, here is my advice on how to avoid looking like a British bloke abroad:

Try to get a bit of a tan on your pasty, white legs before venturing abroad;

Remember to use mosquito repellent before going out in the evenings because those pasty, white legs don't good look with big red blotches all over them;

If you're over twelve, don't wear a football shirt;

Don't wear the type of shirt that's meant to be worn with a suit when you're wearing shorts, especially not with the sleeves rolled down and the cuffs buttoned;

Don't wear the type of shorts that my old Scoutmaster used to wear;

Don't wear those stupid trousers that finish mid-calf and went out of fashion at around the time of Dexy's Midnight Runners;

Don't wear trousers you can unzip and remove the legs so that they may be converted into shorts. I know these may seem like a two-for-one bargain, but, honestly, how much does a separate pair of shorts cost?

Don't wear trainers with "slacks";

In fact, don't wear "slacks". Sean Connery may have looked suave in them as James Bond, but that was in the 1960s. If you absolutely must wear them, choose a colour other than beige;

In fact, don't wear anything beige at all;

Don't wear supermarket own-brand trainers;

Don't tuck your shirt into your shorts unless you're pretending to be an American;

When wearing shorts, don't wear socks that are designed to be worn with trousers;

Don't wear socks with sandals;

Actually, don't wear sandals;

Don't wear one of those wide-brimmed hats of the type favoured by cricket umpires and especially not with the chin-strap fastened.

Just to show that I do, in fact, have a feminine side, here's my advice for the ladies:

If you insist on wearing white trousers or leggings and you are over thirty years old and / or larger than a size ten, please ensure they aren't transparent.

In case you're thinking I'm up my own backside with this advice, I would point out that, although Kim looked gorgeous that evening, I was dressed in the €5 shirt I'd bought in the hypermarket in Bastiagueiro, a pair of Levi's that were in dire need of laundering and my Day Glo trainers, so whilst I didn't look like a tourist, I probably did a good impression of a down-and-out. Kim is fond of telling me that, if she didn't choose my clothes and tell me what to wear, I would look like a "right fuddy-duddy". I'm not exactly sure what a "right fuddy-duddy" looks like, but if it's different to a typical British holidaymaker, I'll gladly settle for it.

As a prelude to the football, a guitarist set up his amplifier close to us and started to sing some songs. He was around my age and played the type of music I enjoy and attempt to play myself. When he came round with his hat, I thanked him and told him I'd enjoyed his set, and we chatted about music for a while. Street entertainers are quite common in Spain and Portugal, but unlike buskers, they tend to make their way round the cafés and restaurants and, after performing a few songs, go round politely inviting the clientele to contribute something towards the entertainment. Kim and I always show our appreciation, even when the quality of the music is total rubbish. We have an old guy in our local town who plays the accordion and sounds as though he's playing one tune with his left hand and another with his right, but he always gets a couple of euros from us for effort.

It always surprises us that, when these performers come round with the hat, the majority of people either totally ignore them as though they don't even exist or dismiss them with a shake their heads. I know that this type of entertainment is thrust upon people rather than requested, but on occasions when we've started to search for some change, we've been told by friends and acquaintances not to encourage them. In fact, some people, who are by no means paupers themselves, have become quite irate about the thought of us giving the musicians any money. Whilst we don't give anything to beggars unless they're obviously in need, as opposed to in need of a bottle of something, we do like to give something to people that have provided some entertainment, on the basis that they're at least doing something to earn the money. In any case, the entertainment adds to the atmosphere, and our opinion is that a couple of euros doesn't amount to much for most people who can afford to sit in a café or restaurant, but it might make a difference to those who are less fortunate, so we're happy to give. Having said that, I'm still not sure whether painting yourself and standing still can be classified as either doing something, or as entertainment, so I tend not to donate anything to "statues", unless they've just made someone shit themselves by suddenly jumping out of statue-mode and yelling at them.

It began to drizzle just before the football started, and Paulo, the singer / guitarist, realising he couldn't compete with the likes of Ronaldo, packed up his gear and wandered over for another chat. He was a friendly guy and seemed to play because he enjoyed it rather than because he needed to earn a living. We invited him to sit with us under the restaurant's large parasol which was doing sterling service as an umbrella. We shared our wine, and as we chatted about music, I soon found that Paolo's and my own musical tastes and influences had a lot in common. When I told him I also played and sang, he handed me his guitar and asked me to do something, probably to see if I was bullshitting or not. I must have done alright because, after a couple of blues numbers, I got a round of applause from the nearby customers. Maybe I should have sent Kim round with the hat. I also probably got a few "shut ups!" from the guys who were trying to listen to the football commentary, but if so, I didn't hear them.

I'm not much of a football fan but, judging by the "oohs" and "ahhs" coming from the crowd in the square, the game must have been exciting. The score was a draw after extra time and ended up in a penalty shoot-out which even I watched with interest. Real Madrid won on penalties, and the Ronaldo connection ensured that the majority of the viewers were happy, so it was a good result all round.

As we strolled (or teetered, in Kim's case) back to the hotel, we passed a double garage attached to a large house. The garage was adjacent to the pavement; the doors were glass-panelled, and the lights had been left on to allow people to see inside. When I stopped for a look, I saw a couple of classic cars set amongst a collection of auto memorabilia. The whole collection was set out and displayed beautifully, and I thought that sharing his passion and beautiful display with passers-by was a splendid thing for the owner to have done.

This random and unusual act of kindness gave me a warm, fuzzy feeling and provided a great end to a really good evening. I liked Cascais a lot.

Day 23, 29 May

Route: Cascais — Lisbon — Silves
Distance today: 290 kilometres (180 miles)
Distance so far: 4,553 kilometres (2,829 miles)
Bike time: 5 hours
Overnight: Casa do Sorro, Silves

We awoke at eight thirty. Kim hadn't slept well. Apparently, someone was snoring again, so I kindly allowed her to have a lie-in whilst I went for coffee in the comfortable and elegant lounge and wrote up my notes from the day before.

We were now only 350 kilometres (218 miles) from home, and it would take us around three and a half hours to get there plus time for any stops along the way. We weren't, however, heading for home. Kim didn't know it yet, but because we hadn't done anything to celebrate her birthday, I'd sneaked onto booking.com and booked an extra night in Silves, which was a place that she'd suggested we visit when we first talked about the trip. Silves is only just over an hour from home, but I wanted to do something special, and I'd found what promised to be a fantastic guesthouse for what was to be our final night on the road.

After saying goodbye to our friendly hosts at the Casa Vela Charm Guesthouse, we were on the road by ten thirty. Satnav Woman guided us out of Cascais and, about twenty minutes later, into Portugal's capital city, Lisbon, where we crossed the mouth of the River Tagus over the Ponte 25 de Abril. This bridge's rich, red colour and design reminded me very much of the San Francisco Golden Gate Bridge which we'd crossed during our USA trip a few years earlier. Unlike the Golden Gate Bridge, this had a couple of lanes that were constructed of open-mesh steel flooring. Motorcycles aren't allowed in these lanes, but as we rode atop the adjacent solid section, the view of the river far below through the open mesh only a couple of feet to the side of Roadie's wheels was disconcerting. Our crossing was overlooked by another plagiarised monument on the far bank. The monument Christ the King shows Jesus with arms outspread and is reminiscent of Christ the Redeemer, the huge statue which dominates Rio de Janeiro. Both bridge and statue were built later than their counterparts in the USA and Brazil, and I thought that, if the Portuguese deliberately set out to plagiarise the originals, then at least they chose some pretty impressive works to copy.

Christ the King watched us impassively as we exited the bridge and entered the A2 motorway which travels in a more or less southerly direction towards the Algarve. I'd previously travelled this road many times en route to Lisbon for my onward flights to Dubai. That was before I worked out that a first-class ticket on the train from Faro for €30 — a journey which talks around the same time as driving — is considerably cheaper than fuel for a thirsty BMW, motorway tolls and long-term airport parking. The motorway is good, and the terrain, although still fairly hilly, was now much flatter than in the north of Portugal. We were in no particular rush, so I was cruising along at around the speed limit of 120 kph (75 mph). Although the weather was sunny, interspersed with cloud, it was quite chilly, and we welcomed the sunny spells when the sun peeped out from behind the clouds and warmed us as we headed towards home — or so Kim thought.

Being in no hurry, we pulled off the motorway looking for a village and coffee, which we soon found, and settled down outside a café on the main street. It was market day, and the place was bustling with vendors touting their wares and local people stocking up on everything from fresh fruit and vegetables to live poultry, old ladies' big pants and weird-looking metal implements that seemed to have no purpose. As we sat enjoying the atmosphere, a looky-looky man wandered from café to café offering trinkets, belts and sunglasses to the patrons. Looky-looky men are of African origin and eke out a living by selling such articles in the markets and on the streets. Their name comes from the fact that their usual patter contains, 'No charge for look,' as they thrust something towards their prospective customers. Any punter foolish enough to take the proffered object will soon find it hard to avoid paying for it because the guy will do anything except take it back and will demand payment. I don't know whether these guys are here legally or not, but I admire the fact they're out there pounding the streets trying to make a living, and I sometimes buy something to try to help them in some small way. Having spent a lot of time in Africa and seen some of the conditions in which people live, in my book, anyone trying to make a better living for themselves deserves a little help along the way.

Back on the road, it was now afternoon, and we were heading south. The weather had turned significantly warmer, and we now were seeing people dressed in T-shirts and shorts, which was something we'd only rarely seen for some time. The landscape had changed from multi-layers of green forest to the brown of agricultural land mixed with wild scrub and greener patches of woods and crops. This was the familiar countryside of the Algarve, and it was beginning to feel as if we were home.

When I headed west at the point where the motorway merges onto the A22 motorway, which shadows the Algarve coast, Kim started thumping my back and shouting at me. Had we been heading home as Kim expected, we should have taken the exit towards the east. I waved, put my finger to my helmet to indicate I couldn't hear what she was saying and carried on riding. She eventually began to realise where we were headed when signs for Silves began to appear, and the thumps turned to a hug and more friendly noises from the pillion.

I'd not been able to persuade Satnav Woman to find either the guesthouse or the road it was situated on, so we rode into the centre of Silves for lunch and to seek directions. I parked the bike next to the car of a Canadian couple who'd just arrived. After complimenting us on Roadie, they told us they were touring Portugal for their honeymoon, and we chatted further. As we exchanged stories and I mentioned the distance we'd covered, the lady said we'd ridden the equivalent of the complete width of Canada. So far, it hadn't occurred to me that we'd done anything exceptional, but it did get me thinking about the distance that we'd ridden.

After lunch at a restaurant situated at the foot of the castle walls, the waiter told us the guesthouse was just outside town, halfway up the hill on the other side of the river, and that we couldn't miss it. Sure enough, as we exited Silves and headed back across the river, we spotted a large building that looked more like a mansion than a guesthouse. The approach was via a steep driveway which ascended the hill diagonally and included a tight hairpin bend to enable the climb to be managed at a sensible gradient.

We were welcomed by George, the proprietor, who invited me to park Roadie in the garage next to his classic 1990's Mercedes SL320. I was amazed to see this car because I have the same model, and during three weeks on the road, I hadn't spotted another SL from this period. Amazingly, here we were, at the end of our trip, parking right next to one in the garage of the guesthouse. It turned out that George was also a Mercedes fan and, as well the modern model which he used as his daily driver, he had another couple of classic Mercedes stored at another location in town. The SL was his wife's car, and she'd owned it from new, so it was a one-careful-lady-owner car of some twenty-something years.

Silves is built along one side of the valley of the Arade river. The

Casa do Sorro guesthouse is situated on the other side of the valley and overlooks a Roman bridge and the town beyond as it rises up the far side of the valley towards the castle. The magnificent vista from the guesthouse's carefully tended and extensive gardens didn't, however, prepare us for the guesthouse itself. George and his wife, Manuela, gave us a guided tour as they showed us to our room, and it soon became apparent from the paintings, artefacts and antiques, a small private chapel and a library full of leather-bound books, that this was less like a guesthouse and more like a museum or stately home. Our room was similarly furnished but also contained a functional en-suite bathroom, which somehow had been constructed and decorated so as not to seem out of place next to our room containing a four-poster bed and beautiful, antique furniture. Whoever had designed and fitted out this place had done a superb job.

After unpacking and changing out of our bike gear, we wandered out to the terrace to seek a bit of sun and a couple of cool beers. George and Manuela joined us and began to explain the history and background of the house and how they came to own it.

George was born in Mozambique and Manuela in Angola, both of which were Portuguese colonies and where their parents were living and working at the time as expats. They met when they returned to Silves — the town where both their families had originated — and they were retired dentists who'd both practised in Silves.

They explained a local artist built the house at the turn of the last century. When I mentioned he must have been a very successful artist to have been able to afford a house like this, George made it clear it was family money rather than artistic talent that built the house. When the artist died, the house stood empty for forty years. George and Manuela always admired the house and would have liked to have bought it, but despite many approaches to the artist's family, the family refused to sell, and the unoccupied house gradually deteriorated into worse and worse condition. Eventually, George and Manuela's persistence paid off, and the family relented, enabling them to purchase it. They spent the next thirty years restoring it to its original condition, furnishing it and spent many hours travelling the length and breadth of Portugal and Spain to find the right furnishings and materials. They'd started offering accommodation around ten months previously and were enjoying sharing the magnificent results of their efforts with their guests. I suspected their motive for letting rooms was more about pride in their achievements than earning an income, and judging by their warm welcome and chatty nature, I think they both enjoyed the company of the guests.

George and Manuela were soon obliged to excuse themselves to welcome some new arrivals who, having checked in and been given the grand tour, joined us on the terrace where we shared a bottle of wine. Bernard and Liz were from Ireland and, although they had a holiday home nearby, had come to stay at Casa do Sorro to check it out and to see if it matched its growing local reputation.

After an enjoyable hour or so chatting with our fellow guests, Kim and I strolled down the hill and over the Roman bridge into town. Bernard and Liz had recommended a bar that had live music and would be holding an open-mike night that evening. The food wasn't up to much, but the music was entertaining with many people joining in, and there were some talented musicians taking part. I was tempted to ask if I could do a couple of numbers. By this time, however, I'd had quite a lot to drink, but not enough not to realise that, without playing much recently and with quite a bit of booze on board, I would probably not do very well. I sensibly, and much to Kim's relief, refrained from volunteering a contribution to the evening's entertainment.

The last day of our trip and Kim's belated birthday celebrations had been very enjoyable.

Day 23, 29 May • 231

On the road in Portugal

Day 24, 30 May

Route: Silves — Home
Distance today: 115 kilometres (71 miles)
Distance so far: 4,668 kilometres (2,901 miles)
Bike time: 1 hours 15 minutes
Overnight: Home

We awoke to bright, blue skies and warm temperatures. When we went down to breakfast, Manuela said that, according to the forecast, the weather was going to be fine and hot for several days. This was just what we wanted to hear on the last day of a trip that had seen us experience rain on twelve of the twenty-four days that we'd been on the road.

I liked George and Manuela's breakfast arrangements. Instead of individual tables for the guests, we were all seated at a long dining table, an arrangement which encouraged the guests to chat and interact with one another over breakfast. Bernard and Liz joined us along with another friendly couple from Scotland and all enjoyed a leisurely breakfast, exchanging stories with each other and with George and Manuela.

Having returned to our wonderful room to change into our riding gear and to finish packing, we were on the road by quarter to eleven. With only 115 kilometres (71 miles) to ride, we would be home in just over an hour. Kim had thoroughly enjoyed the extra surprise night in Silves, and we'd both loved George and Manuela and their wonderful guesthouse. My guilt at neglecting to do anything to celebrate Kim's birthday had been well and truly assuaged and, hopefully, I may even have gained a couple of "good husband" points.

Our route was along the A22 motorway which, although situated several kilometres inland, roughly follows the Algarve coastline. We had to stop for gas at Loule, but instead of staying for our usual coffee, we mounted straight up and headed for home. Kim didn't say anything, but I could tell she was itching to get there, probably to start cleaning the house she'd cleaned immediately before we left, or to start one of the projects she'd no doubt been thinking about during the hours she'd been sitting behind me on the bike. As we rode along, I caught a smell of pine trees. Pines surround our house, and this familiar scent made me feel as if I was home already. I wound on the throttle a little, and after turning off the motorway just before the bridge into Spain, we pulled up outside our house at twelve o'clock exactly.

Over the next few days, I began to put my notes of the trip in order. The Canadian lady's comment in Silves that we'd ridden the equivalent of the entire width of Canada on our trip (I found out after checking that this was a little overstated, because we were around 1,000 kilometres [620 miles] short), made me begin to think that what had started as a loose plan to tour Spain and Portugal could actually have been an achievement worthy of some note. I don't mean for one moment to compare what we'd done to those adventure riders who've covered huge distances in remote areas, spent months on the road or those who've crossed whole continents, but I began to think it was something to be proud of, and I gathered some statistics.

We'd ridden a total of 4,668 kilometres (2,901 miles). Compare this to the following notable journeys:

Land's End to John O'Groats — 1,093 kilometres (679 miles). We'd ridden more than four times this distance.
London to Rome — 1,833 kilometres (1,139 miles). This is only forty per cent of the distance of our trip.
New York to Miami — 2,059 kilometres (1,279 miles) — about half our distance.
London to Istanbul (where Europe ends and Asia starts) — 2,988 kilometres (1,857 miles). We'd travelled almost 1,700 kilometres (1,000 miles) further than the Orient Express.
Sydney to Perth (the width of Australia) — 3,939 kilometres (2,448 miles). Oz is a big country, and this is an epic route, but we'd ridden further.
Chicago to Los Angeles via Route 66 — 3,940 kilometres (2,448 miles). We'd ridden 700 kilometres (450 miles) further that this famous road.

As you can see, the distance of our trip was greater than all of these, which made me wonder how we'd achieved such a long distance without really realising it. One thing that hadn't really struck home to me before is the sheer size of the Iberian Peninsula. Geographically speaking, Great Britain is the main island that makes up mainland United Kingdom, and it has an area of 210,000 square kilometres (81,000 square miles). Spain, Andorra and Portugal have a combined area of around 598,000 square kilometres (231,000 square miles) which is a whopping 2.8 times bigger than Great Britain. It's fairly obvious, therefore, that to circumnavigate the Iberian Peninsula requires a good distance to be travelled.

We'd discovered that, in the same way that the extreme points of Britain that are found in Cornwall, Pembrokeshire, Caithness and Norfolk are vastly different in terms of terrain, climate, architecture, character, regional language and / or accent, the various regions of Spain and Portugal each have their own rich and varied characteristics. We'd thoroughly enjoyed this diversity from the big city of Barcelona to the remoteness of some of the Furthest Points, so much so that it was difficult to pick our favourite places because so many of them, each in their unique way had had so much to recommend them.

We'd reconfirmed our belief that, in general, the Spanish and Portuguese are friendly and hospitable people, and this is especially so if you take the trouble to speak their language. You don't have to be perfect, or even to be very good at it, but your efforts are very much appreciated and will very often lead to friendly encounters, funny conversations and lots of smiles.

After so many years of staying in expensive and impersonal hotels on business, mainly in large cities, it was fantastic for me to discover, thanks to Kim-Dot-Com, that very individual, comfortable and friendly accommodation is available at very reasonable prices in Spain and Portugal. The average we paid for a night's accommodation was only €80, and the standard of the accommodation for the entire trip was such that we wouldn't hesitate to return to any of the places where we stayed. I, for one, would prefer to stay in most of the places we found on our trip than the sterile, impersonal accommodation in Dubai and such places, 5-stars or otherwise.

In many ways, the trip also reflected our life as expatriates. We didn't have much of a plan for the trip except to visit Yasmin and David and to try to visit the Furthest Points. How we would get there? What we would do on the way? Where would we stay? Would we make it in the allotted time? All these things would be entirely dependent on circumstances along the way. We never really had a plan during our life overseas either, except to make a reasonable living whilst enjoying life as a family. Consequently, for most of the time, we enjoyed living in the places to which the road of life had taken us, and we moved on when we either stopped enjoying things or new opportunities presented themselves. Who knows whether

Portugal will be our last destination or whether we will ever return to the UK to live? We never say never.

Apart from a few bikeless years when the family came along, biking has been a part of my life since I was fourteen and too young to hold a licence. I can honestly say that, even when I've been soaking wet, cold, tired and miserable on a bike, I've never once considered giving up biking. I've enjoyed riding bikes, working on bikes, customising bikes and dreaming about bikes, and I've particularly enjoyed the fact that, for the past several years, biking has been something Kim and I have been able to share. Over the years, I've ridden motorcycles in seventeen different countries, and on most of these occasions, Kim has been with me. It's been a fantastic way for us to discover new countries and to experience all that goes with this type of travel. Motorcycling has also enabled us to meet many new people through the biking community, many of whom have become good friends. We've laughed a lot, drunk a lot and partied a lot as well as ridden a lot in the company of many, many good people, all due to biking.

During our trip, we spent a total of twenty-four days on the road and, for the vast majority of that time, Kim and I were in each other's company for twenty-four hours a day, seven days a week. I'm not saying we didn't get a little tetchy with each other on occasion, but from my point of view at least, this was reconfirmation that I'd made an excellent choice when I asked Kim to marry me thirty-odd years ago. The Wrong-Way-Round trip could also be said to have many parallels with the time Kim and I have been together. We had many fantastic days on the trip, but we also had some miserable times when the weather or other factors were against us, but we never once wanted to give up in the face of a few challenges. Kim and I have often had to dig deep to overcome various challenges during our life together, and in the same way that we went the extra mile to extend our time on the road to complete the trip, we always worked together and supported each other to make things right. We thoroughly enjoyed the whole experience and our time together.

It wasn't a bad trip either!

238 • THE FURTHEST POINTS

Cabo de Roca, Furthest Point West (Mainland Europe)

Postscript

Do you remember how this book opened? We were on the road to Ronda when the bike refused to go round a right-hand bend and drifted to the left side of the road. I spent many weeks thinking and worrying about this and trying to work out what had happened and why, but I'd failed to find any feasible reason except for rider error. Several months after our trip, in the early morning before the golfers were out and about, I was jogging round the golf course which is conveniently situated at the bottom of our garden. It was raining, and the buggy track round which I was running was wet. As I climbed up a particularly steep section, I felt my trainers slip on the tarmac. Looking down at the surface, which was wet and shiny with the moisture, it suddenly seemed very familiar. The stones embedded in the tarmac had the same smooth, slippery look as those on the road to Ronda. I slid my trainers along the surface, and sure enough, there was a lot less grip than I would have expected.

Maybe my gut feeling at the time of the incident was correct, and the whole bike had slid sideways on both tyres. If this was the case, then my instinctive feeling at the time had been correct. If I'd laid the bike down further to make it turn tighter, the tyres would have lost all traction, and we would have ended up on the floor, or over the side of the cliff.

I can't say for sure, but I prefer this version to the rubbish-rider alternative.

Appendix A

Packing for a Three-Week Motorcycle Trip

As promised, here is a list of the stuff we took on the trip. This was all decided on as a result of previous, extended road trips. I hope it helps if you're planning a similar trip.

Andy
Riding Gear

- US shorty, cop helmet
- Earplugs
- Oakley sunglasses (also used as off-bike sunglasses)
- Oakley clear riding glasses
- Neck warmer
- Harley-Davidson Switchback jacket
- Frank Thomas medium-weight bike gloves
- Bull-It waterproof, Kevlar-lined jeans
- Hiking socks — 2 pairs
- Dr. Martens boots
- Frank Thomas rain jacket and pants

Andy
Off-Bike Gear

- Climalite T-shirts — 3
- T-shirts — 3

Long-sleeved, thermal shirt

Thin fleece (also used for extra insulation under bike jacket)

Rugby shirt (Barbarians, if you must know)

Casual shirt

Jeans

Casual shorts

Sports / swimming shorts

Socks — 2 pairs

Sports socks — 2 pairs

Undies — 4 pairs

Toilet bag and toiletries

Laptop (for keeping up with work)

Notebook (you don't think I just remembered all the stuff for this book, do you?)

Kim

Riding Gear

Harley-Davidson half helmet with visor

Bandana

Harley-Davidson jacket

Jeans (also used for off-bike wear)

Cagoule, used as waterproof jacket

Waterproof pants

Dr. Martens boots

Kim

Off-Bike Gear

Climalite sports shirt

Sleeveless top

Smart, long-sleeved top

T-shirts — 5

Bras — 2

Sports bra

Sweatpants

Sports shorts

Bikini

Sports socks — 3 pairs

Sandals (trendy and not Brit-abroad style)

High heels (she may be a biker babe, but she has class)

Pashmina (also used for extra riding insulation)

Toiletries and makeup

Joint Stuff

Mac charger

iPad

iPad charger and cable

Phones

Phone charger and cable

Credit cards

Camera

Passports

Michelin road atlas of Spain and Portugal

Bike Stuff

Garmin zūmo 660

Tool roll (not used)

First aid kit (not used)

Tyre gunk aerosol (not used)

Bike documents

Appendix B

Statistics

Here are a few facts and figures from our trip. If you're planning a similar trip, I hope you'll find this useful.

Total distance travelled: 4,668 kilometres (2,901 miles)

Furthest distance in one day: 506 kilometres (314 miles) — home to Ronda

Shortest distance in one day: 115 kilometres (72 miles) — Silves to home

Average distance per riding day: 275 kilometres (171 miles)

Number of days spent on the trip: 24

Riding days: 17

Non-riding days: 7

Total hours riding: 78

Most hours riding per day: 7 hours 30 minutes — home to Ronda

Fewest hours riding per day: 1 hour 15 minutes — Silves to home

Average hours riding per riding day: 4 hours 35 minutes

Most expensive hotel: €133 — Hotel Condal Mar, Barcelona

Least expensive hotel: €42 — Aparthotel Attica21 As Galeras, Bastiagueiro

Average cost of accommodation: €80 (not including free accommodation with Yasmin and David)

Cost of fuel: €362

Number of rainy days: 12 (I think we were unlucky, as this isn't typical in this region for May)

Number of dickheads encountered: 2

Number of nice people encountered: Many

Contact the Author

I sincerely thank you for reading this book and hope you enjoyed it. It would mean a lot to me if you would leave a review on Amazon.

I'd love to hear your comments and am happy to answer any questions you may have. Do please get in touch with me by:

Email: andy.hewitt.books@gmail.com

Facebook: www.facebook.com/andy.hewitt.73

I look forward to hearing from you.

Andy Hewitt

Acknowledgements

My thanks go to the following people:

Yasmin and David for accommodation, lovely dinners, sausage sandwiches and being great mates. David also kindly produced the map of our route and the Furthest Points which appears in Appendix B.

Jacky Donovan for editing, much advice and helping me through the whole self-publishing process.

Biker mates whose company and friendship I have enjoyed, however fleetingly, over the years.